WAGING WAR ON FEAR

Strategies to Overcome a Scary World

WAGING WAR ON FEAR

Strategies
to Overcome
a Scary World

BETTY PARKER

WINEPRESS **WP** PUBLISHING

Packaged by WinePress Publishing, PO Box 428, Enumclaw, WA 98022. The views expressed or implied in this work do not necessarily reflect those of WinePress Publishing. The author(s) is ultimately responsible for the design, content, and editorial accuracy of this work.

Unless otherwise noted, all scriptures are taken from the Holy Bible, New International Version, Copyright © 1973, 1978, 1984 by the International Bible Society. Used by permission of Zondervan Publishing House. The "NIV" and "New International Version" trademarks are registered in the United States Patent and Trademark Office by International Bible Society.

ISBN 1-57921-476-2

Library of Congress Catalog Card Number: 2002106169

Dedication:

To my miracle baby, Justice

Contents

Acknowledgments

All praises and honor are due to the Lord God Almighty for giving me a story to tell that is both tragic and triumphant. I'd also like to acknowledge the support of my husband, Reggie, for his encouragement and love. A very special thank you to my sister, Deb, who forced me to explore the deeper understanding of what I went through so I could share it in this book. Much gratitude to Diane Johnson for being my "editor" and for always supporting my writing dream. A big hug to my sisters, Pauline and Wanda, for encouraging my spiritual growth and development because we love to preach good news to one another! I am most appreciative to my pastor, Rev. Dr. Charles B. Jackson Sr., who told me that I *must* share this story.

I can't thank the doctors at South Carolina OB/GYN enough for their excellent care during my extended stay in the hospital. I offer much gratitude to the high risk nursing staff at Palmetto Baptist Medical Center in Columbia, S.C.—Terry, Myra, Francena—you're angels! A big thank you to the NICU staff and especially to Jill Lester, RN, who is a saint. Thanks for the PhotoParade! To the doctors and staff at the REACH clinic and the Institute for Assisted Reproduction in Charlotte, N.C., The Center for Women's Medicine, and Dr. Gail Whitman-Elia, thank you for your concern and prayers. Thanks to Carolinas Medical Center and CARS for the cards and calls, and to Joan Schertz for being a woman of faith and sharing it. To Renice, Meredith, and Dan for reading the rough, rough drafts and offering your undying support, thank you.

And to every blessed soul who visited me in the hospital, called, brought me food, and offered prayers and encouraging words, I am forever grateful for your thoughtfulness and acts of kindness. May God continue to bless you all.

Introduction

D o you remember the times when you were deeply engrossed in a particular task and didn't pay much attention to what was going on around you? You were focused solely on what you were doing at the moment and blocked out your surroundings. Then out of nowhere someone jumped out of the shadows and roared at you or even yelled, "Boo!" Depending on how crafty they were, they probably caught you completely off guard and scared the grits out of you. To them, it was hilarious. And after the shock wore off, you, too, found that it was funny. You were shaky with relief after you realized that it was only a prank. But boy, were you ever frightened when it happened!

We've all been there, and we've even pulled the same prank on someone else. Remember what you had to do to plan it? You had to hide. You had to be very quiet. You surveilled your target closely to determine the best time to strike. And you relished the outcome. What makes such a prank most effective is being able to catch the person totally off guard. Timing is critical because you must find the moment when the person is most vulnerable and totally unsuspecting.

That's how life comes at us sometimes. We can be going about our daily routines, caught up in the monotony of it all, and then, "Boo!"

From out of nowhere, tragedy strikes, and our lives suddenly spiral out of control. We are immediately bewildered, upset, and—most of all— *scared*. We don't know what to do. And in many cases, we soon discover that we can do very little. We are vulnerable.

Such was the state of my life in 2001. It was a time I now call "the Year of Fear." I was cruising along as happy as a lark (I could have perched in a tree and sung a song). My life was full, blessed, and abundant with great opportunities on the way. I anticipated many exciting things ahead of me. And then, without warning, out of the shadows came a roar— "Boo!" My heart did a free fall and landed hard in the pit of my stomach. I was petrified. This was no harmless joke; this was real. A prank lasts for only a few moments and is over. Afterward, everybody shares a good laugh and moves on. But this fear lasted longer than a moment. In fact, it seemed as though it would never end. Days, even weeks, and eventually months passed.

I dubbed 2001 "the Year of Fear" because I was not only struggling with my own personal fears but was catapulted into new fears, along with the rest of the nation. The September 11 terrorist attacks on the World Trade Centers and the Pentagon made fear an archenemy of mine and most of the country. I had never before considered it my foe because I can't remember ever being that frightened. But when I finally recognized fear as my true enemy, I fought it. Oh what a war that waged between us! It gave me a licking, but I was the one still standing when the bell rung.

After I won, I reflected on how I had made it through without defeat. I later discovered that I'd implemented specific strategies that gained me the victory—strategies of which I had not been aware while I was in combat. I believe that they were God-inspired, Spirit-led, and Jesus taught. I can give no one else the credit. What happened in my life was nothing short of a miracle. I'm sure that you'll agree as you read my story. I believe that miracles must be shared. I believe that it is especially pertinent now more than ever. God must be glorified in this time when evil seems to be gaining the upper hand.

Thus was born the purpose for this book. My goal in writing it is to spread spiritual knowledge and to empower you against your enemy when that enemy is fear. No matter what scares you, I believe that you can fight fear and end the war with your foot upon its neck. Even if you have lived in fear so long that you can't remember when it started, you can read these strategies with the expectation that they are a proven plan for winning. You can *finally* be released from fear. You can have the confidence that if you prepare your heart and mind to receive this message, you will emerge the victor. The battle against fear is unlike any physical battle that you have fought. This is spiritual warfare, the toughest kind of fight. You can break a man's back in battle and paralyze him, rendering him helpless. But if you don't break his spirit, he can still prevail.

In this book, you will find answers. *You can prevail.* Expect a revelation. Most importantly, prepare to be moved to action. I am excited about what God showed me in my battles. And because I followed the strategies that He mapped out for me, I did not taste defeat. Rather, I found joy and peace.

Do you know peace? It is the friend that awaits you when your enemy fear has been forced to retreat.

Please read this short book with hope, understanding, and courage. And may the peace of the Lord be yours always.

The Gift of Peace

Peace I leave with you; my peace I give you. I do not give to you as the world gives. Do not let your hearts be troubled and do not be afraid. (John 14:27)

I have told you these things, so that in me you may have peace. In this world you will have trouble. But take heart! I have overcome the world. (John 16:33)

Chapter One

The Fight for "Justice"

Remember how "Y2K" was the annoying buzz in 1999, and people were afraid that all kinds of things would go crazy? There were predictions that the world would come to an end, Christ would return, or mankind would be devastated in any number of ways. Much fear was circulating around the globe. But the year 2000 came in like a lamb and was so uneventful that we hardly noticed its departure.

After the new millennium arrived without incident, the world seemed to let out a collective sigh. However, 2001 rolled in, and a new level of fear debuted. It waited until we had let down our guard, and then it joined forces with evil and struck us. The country would not face this monster until September, but it jumped out of the shadows at me in April. The story I'm about to share with you was the most frightening experience I've ever had. It is by no means unique in itself; albeit, it was certainly unique for me. Many women have gone through the same agony that I endured–and worse. I feel compelled, however, to share my story out of a commitment that I made to God. I also feel apprehensive.

After hearing my story, some readers will probably say, "So what?" They've had it a lot worse. Why should I think that my experience was any more frightening than theirs? But I've come to understand that it's not so much the uniqueness of the story as the lessons learned from it that matter most. What God taught me in my struggle might be different than the lessons of another woman in a similar situation. And although many other pilgrims have trekked this road before me, I could find hardly anyone with whom to discuss the experience in depth when I most needed answers and direction. I needed a game plan for how I could get to the end a winner.

Unfortunately, a clear-cut strategy was not easy to find; it was virtually nonexistent. The women to whom I spoke and who had been where I was had promised to pray for me. I know they did because the results are astounding. But I needed something between those prayers, something that, until the end came, would bring me comfort. Sure, I had faith. But my faith was being tested by the hour, the day, the week, and eventually even the month. *Where* could I turn in my weakest moments to be strengthened?

I went to God. I prayed and sought out His Holy Word. He answered. He provided me with the courage and wisdom that I needed to face each difficult day and each arduous night. Every time fear landed a blow, the Lord was in my corner, coaching me on how to bounce back from it. James tells us that if we ask for wisdom, God will give it to us generously (James 1:5). The revelations that He provided were overwhelming. He shared seven strategies with me on how to defeat fear. I tried them, and they worked. Now I will share them with you. I believe that the Lord desires that we be informed, that we all be made wiser. You can learn from my hardships, and someone else can learn from yours. As believers, we must stand as a united front against any and all evil. So out of obedience, here's my story.

On April 12, 2001, I was packing for a trip back to my home town in Louisiana to spend Easter with my family. I had to catch a plane early the next morning to New Orleans. I was 23 weeks pregnant with my first child, and everyone back home was excited. I was excited too and was looking forward to showing off my growing belly. When I finally settled down to bed that night, I hardly got the chance to close my eyes before the unthinkable happened. Without a warning, my membranes ruptured, or, in more common terminology, my water broke. It gushed from my body like a garden hose, and in minutes, I was standing in a puddle of fluid in my bedroom. I could not stop it, and it was one of the most helpless feelings I'd ever experienced. There would be more to come.

"Oh no!" I told my husband. "This is not supposed to be happening. Not now!"

As we scurried around the house in a panic trying to get dressed and to the hospital, the fluid continued to pour. It was a sickening feeling. It was like watching someone die and not being able to do a thing about it. After all, this water was protecting the unborn life within me. It had already contributed a great deal to his survival. *Will this baby die?* I wondered. With my limited knowledge of pregnancy, I thought that it would indeed. I thought that this event meant the end of my first attempt to bear a child. I was simultaneously devastated, horrified, and confused. I could not fathom experiencing such a loss this far into the pregnancy. I had seen the baby flip around on ultrasound. I had watched the growth of his tiny spine; both hemispheres of his brain; and his tiny legs, arms, hands, and feet. I'd heard his rapid heartbeat and saw his male parts.

My husband and I had been ecstatic about this new life that I carried inside of me. This was our first child together. This baby had become a critical part of us—especially me. It was as though this little guy had given *me* life instead of the other way around. But he was not due to make his debut until August 10. He still had so much growth ahead of him. He was 16 weeks away from term. He couldn't survive this early in life without my womb to nurture his development.

These thoughts raced through my head. But the greater message, which I ignored, raced through my heart.

It would be several months after my son's birth before I'd realize that deep within my spirit God had already told me that He would not permit the death of my child. I knew it immediately, even as I rummaged around my armoire for clothes. I should have stopped, embraced the encouragement of the Holy Spirit, and relaxed. But fear made me push aside God's assurances and told me that I should panic. Doom was on its way.

When my husband got me to the hospital, the medical personnel took me to triage and set me up behind a curtain of thin fabric that separated me from other expectant moms. I could hear fetal monitors as they sounded out the babies' rapid heartbeats. In the weeks to come, I would come to hate those monitors although they are vitally important for pregnant women. I heard the mother behind the curtain next to mine speaking to her doctor about whether she should stay overnight or come back later. Her baby was due in four days, but she was having contractions now. My baby was due in four *months*! How I envied her dilemma.

Eventually the doctor who was on call for me came in with an ultra-sound machine. He wanted to see how much amniotic fluid still surrounded the baby. The amniotic fluid provided a sterile environment where the baby lived and moved, and it was essential for his survival. It acted as a shock absorber from the contractions of my uterus. It protected him and me from infection and other life-threatening possibilities. The doctor searched and searched, but he could find no fluid. The image of the baby was no longer distinct. Without the fluid, the picture was grainy and difficult to discern. I began to feel that I was already losing touch with my baby. He was fading away.

The doctor sat next to me on the edge of the bed and looked at me gravely. "You are in a very terrible situation," he said.

I knew that his words were true, and my heart plummeted at the sound of them. I was convinced that I had lost the baby. The doctor didn't give me much hope. He told us what to expect—which wasn't much. Babies this young have a low survival rate if they are delivered this early. And even if my baby did live, he would face a multitude of physical problems. My husband had been holding his *Daily Walk Living Bible* as he sat next to my bed. The doctor noticed it. He told my husband that reading the Word was the best thing he could do. There was not much to be done medically.

The doctor left my bedside, and my husband joined him. I felt lonely and disoriented. I forced myself not to ask why, but I was bewildered by all that was taking place. I thought that God wanted me to have this baby. I had consulted Him about it long before I tried to get pregnant. And I thought that He had approved because He had granted me this little gift. Why would He take him away? Did God really work that way? I knew He didn't, but I couldn't help wondering if the demise of this pregnancy was His will. I knew that He enjoys giving gifts to us, His children. His Word tells us so.

"Which of you, if his son asks for bread, will give him a stone? Or if he asks for a fish, will give him a snake? If you then, though you are evil, know how to give good gifts to your children, how much more will your Father in heaven give good gifts to those who ask Him!" (Matt. 7:9–11)

Hadn't God given all of us the ultimate gift of His only Son, Jesus Christ? His love for us is so vast and deep that He offered up His own child as a sacrifice for us. How many of us would do the same? But some readers might say, "Well, I lost a child. Where was His compassion then?" Or "Why does God permit so many children to die if He's so loving?"

I believe there are two reasons. First, many children die at the hands of others—most of whom are their parents. If you decided right now to harm your or anyone else's child, you might very well succeed if no one were around to stop you. But that would be a choice that *you* made, not God. And you will be held accountable for that action. Sometimes God intervenes; sometimes He doesn't. I don't know how He makes His choice on when to step in, but He will hold any person who commits such an unspeakable act responsible. Be careful not to blame God for the actions of the wicked.

Second, even if you are a loving parent who suffered the loss of a child, and you think that you did everything you could to save your child, take heart. Your loss and suffering and the circumstances surrounding it were not a wasted event designed to leave you tortured and broken. The answer lies in your relationship with God. He will sometimes use our children—our most prized possessions—to do His work, even in their infancy.

For example, a wonderful woman who works with me endured a harrowing experience with her grandson who was diagnosed with a rare cancer at the tender age of nine months. The first couple of years of his precious life were fraught with surgeries, pain, chemotherapy, sickness, and various other side effects. The family suffered as much as he did, watching their tiny baby as he faced horrendous hardship. My coworker often e-mailed me and others about his progress. I noticed that her e-mails went to dozens of people. She sometimes forwarded e-mails from her daughter to us. Attached to her daughter's message would be dozens more names. This baby's story went out all over the country. Through his affliction, this little boy captured the hearts of hundreds of people. Among that number, many people might not have prayed if not for that child. Some of them might not have spoken to God much at all before they were touched by his trauma. That one tiny infant brought a great number of people together in communion with God, and when he was cured, God received the glory. He answered their prayers, and the evidence was before them in the precious saved life of this little boy.

The bundle of joy that we birth might be an angel brought here for a short time to do God's work. No child is ours forever. They're all on loan. Some of them might be with us for only a little while, and they might seem to be sick and suffering almost the entire time they are here. But we must look deeper than their apparent discomfort or loss.

Once when my mother was critically ill, I thought that she was suffering, but she told me later that she had no recollection of the agony in which I'd seen her. God is merciful! Survey the circumstances around your child's life and/or death. Look at the entire landscape, not just the one mountain before you. What mark did your child leave behind? What was his or her short legacy? Whose life was touched and changed as a result? Do not allow your grief to cause you to overlook the blessing that the birth of that child brought. Consider yourself blessed to be chosen by God to have born one of His angels.

Even if you have miscarried and have never had the chance to give birth, that unborn baby served the same purpose. These views are only my beliefs. The One who is best able to answer your questions is God the Father Himself. Ask Him. And remember that one day, we'll all get the chance to see Him face to face and get direct responses. Until then, I was sure that He had a reason for the ordeal that I faced. I asked God to reveal to me what He wanted me to know.

While the doctor and my husband were gone, I lay praying to God for the strength to face whatever the outcome would be. I begged Him to spare my child's life. I reminded Him that I had consulted Him before trying to conceive. Then He reminded me that He *is God* who answers prayer. He'd given me what I wanted, but He didn't say that it would be a breeze. I would come to appreciate this blessing above all others.

I guess it was the way in which fear came at me that made me believe at first its threats above God's promises. Fear threw me a sucker punch. The ordeal happened suddenly; I never saw it coming. And when it hit me, it knocked me down. And while I was down, it kept pummeling and kicking me. So often I've heard people say, "God never gives you more than you can bear." I now take issue with that statement. This situation was way more than I could stand! I was beaten down and feeling nearly destroyed. But a profound lesson was implanted in me that has grown roots. I came to realize that I was taken to a breaking point because that limit forced me to give up all that I thought I could control and surrender completely to God. At first, I didn't surrender readily, so I suffered a great deal through this fight. Growing into wiser, more dedicated disciples is challenging and even painful. But we must

23

never lose sight of the priceless lessons and rewards that are ours when the bell rings and the fight is over.

Romans 5:3–5 tells us how to view our hardships: "Not only so, but we also rejoice in our sufferings, because we know that suffering produces perseverance; perseverance, character; and character, hope. And hope does not disappoint us because God has poured out His love into our hearts by the Holy Spirit, whom He has given us."

I know that it is difficult to show joy when you are afraid, angry, or hurting. But as we trudge through our sufferings, we are increasing our endurance. Every time we get through one crisis, we are being prepared and strengthened to handle the next crisis—but even better. It is like training for a marathon of which I've run a couple. To complete the 26.2-mile run, I had to push myself farther and farther against—and beyond—formidable barriers that I'd already conquered. One week, a long run was fifteen miles on a Saturday morning. The next long run had to be sixteen miles. Even if I stepped back a mile one week and ran a mile less, the following week I would go beyond the previous limit. My body was being conditioned to endure. And so it should be with our spirits. We should condition our spirits to overcome during the trying times so that when they come again (and they will), we will still prevail—even more successfully than we did the previous time.

We persevere, and we evolve. Every challenge should bring about a change for the better in us. Having learned valuable life lessons, we should renew ourselves when it's over. Our stronger character should lead us to hope in all things. Having been through and overcome, we should have greater hope in God, the Holy Spirit, answered prayer, and ourselves. We should never surrender to defeat despite the outcome. Above all, we should always know that God loves us. I reminded myself of this fact as I readied myself for my duel with fear.

So I embarked on a journey of forty days of testing. They would be dark, fretful, scary, and agonizing. I am so glad that I didn't know what was ahead because I would surely have fainted at the thought. I lay in triage and reflected on how the situation could have gotten to this point.

Was it because I'd angered Satan by boasting about how wonderfully blessed I was? My life was abundant and fulfilling. Everything was rolling along smoothly. I was content with the present and excited about the future. And I glorified God in it all. I think Satan was miffed, so he decided to wreck a few things.

This was his strategy: release fear—one of his strongest contenders—upon me. He apparently thought that my gratitude toward God's goodness would be short-lived if I had to face heartache and devastation. Would I brag about the Lord's greatness when my happy, little life took a nosedive? It's easy to praise Him when all is well. Would I feel the same when a precious part of me was threatened?

Suddenly, I had become Job. Satan had asked God's permission to tempt me, to put me to a test. Did I have the stuff of true Christians, or would I crack under pressure? He bargained with God to let him send out his prizefighter, fear, and let it attack what was most precious to me. That would do it. That was the way to break a Christian. In his devious yet faulty thinking, Satan thought that I'd turn on the Lord in anger. But he couldn't have been more wrong. Instead of driving me away from God, he only drove me closer to Him.

Often, in our pain, we get angry with God. We think that He lets us down because He allows tragedy to come into our lives. We might give up on Him or turn our backs on Him because we think that He has abandoned us. We humans are fickle that way. But God is always committed to us if we trust in Him. I'm glad that He doesn't abandon us as readily as we reject Him. Instead of becoming resentful, we must take action. This is the time when we must try our hardest to put aside emotions and use our intelligence. Research the Word of God and learn His will. He often uses these opportunities to test us. That's what He did to me. He put me to the test—not to see if I'd pass or fail but to increase my knowledge of His power and the power that He gives me. In my hospital room, I committed to Him my love for Him and trust in Him no matter what.

I said, "Lord, I don't understand why this turn of events has occurred, but I've known you too long to doubt you. I've been blessed by you too often to think that you'll let me down. You've shown your love for me over and over again, and I commit my love to you. Whatever the outcome, let me stand strong in the end. I commend everything I am to you."

I stared into the darkness and reasoned that God had given His only Son for me. How dare I not be willing to give my son if it was His desire to have him? Could this be how Mary felt when she had to accept the fact that Jesus would be murdered to accomplish the will of the Father? Yielding to His will is sometimes agonizing, but we must fight to do so. Besides, who was I to think that I could stop God from taking my son if He wanted to? I was a grieving mother, that's who—a grieving mother who was appealing to a compassionate God to grant the live, healthy birth of her unborn child. And God listens to those pleas.

We can convince Him through fervent prayer to meet our wishes. After all, why pray if you don't expect to have your petitions granted? He gives us that privilege. The tricky part comes in praying for those things that are in line with His will for us. Jesus said that we should pray, "Thy will be done." And just because we are praying for something that *we* perceive as being good does not mean that we get those prayers answered automatically. I'll say it again: the success of our prayers being answered rests in God's will for us. Because I did not yet know His will, I became afraid.

I didn't know why God had chosen my child and me to endure this hardship, but I prayed that He wouldn't take my son. I reminded the Lord of all of the promises He'd made in His Word. I prayed constantly and reverently, making my requests in the name of Jesus. When I learned long ago that the key to having my prayers granted rested in the name of Jesus, I began to invoke its power mightily. His name has irrevocable power. He has given it to us and will not take it back. All I had to do was ask in His Name, believe, and not doubt (Mark 11:23–24). Doubt is fueled by fear, so I fought it as though it was as great an enemy as the

Devil himself. And it is as great an enemy because Satan's the one who creates fear to destroy our faith.

This point brings us to Strategy #1 as we plan to wage war against fear: "Expose your enemy and stand up against it. Never run." First, we have to identify the real culprit to defeat it. I didn't readily recognize fear as my enemy. He was slick and cunning, and I was misled. But that's how Satan works. When he dispatches his evil spirits such as fear, he cleverly disguises them. Fear was able to perform all kinds of devious acts against me because I didn't recognize it. And because I didn't know how to combat it, it immediately got the upper hand. I blamed myself because I believed that I'd allowed my faith to wane. But God revealed the truth to me, and my failing wasn't at issue; rather, it was the evil plots of fear. This is what fear did.

> **Strategy #1**
> Expose your enemy and stand up against it. Never run.

The next day, it came into my room with the neonatologist and smirked as the doctor delivered the terrible news. He said that if I had to deliver that day, my baby's viability would not be good. Babies born at twenty-three weeks had only about a 50 percent chance of survival. And if my child did survive, he would be at risk for many complications. Statistics also indicated that 70 percent of the women in my condition usually delivered within seven to ten days. The odds were stacked against me.

I felt a profound feeling of helplessness once again. I felt let down and disappointed. By whom—God? Dare I say it? It was exactly what Satan wanted to hear. But the loss of the baby was not supposed to happen. Everything had been going along well. God had answered my prayers for a child. Didn't He want me to have one? Why would He change His mind? I refused to think that the God Who had brought me this far would abandon me now. He had to have some purpose for this alteration in plans. Once again, I prayed that He would show me what it was.

My heart was filled with alarm and apprehension as I lay in bed. I could hardly hold up my head. I'd never known such fear before, and I knew that neither the doctors nor I nor anyone else could change things. Not physically anyway. This was a spiritual thing. This situation was entirely in the hands of God. No one other than He could help me. No one. Now I had to relinquish everything within me that sought control and become totally dependent on Him. That was a difficult task because I had to function on faith alone. I had to take God at His Word. If only I knew what His Word was regarding this particular situation. He hadn't yet made Himself clear on it. So I was afraid, and an ugly cycle was set in motion. Fear led to worry and worry to doubt. Doubt weakened me and led me back to fear. And it went around and around like that. I had a heavy load to bear. I wanted to get rid of my fears, but I couldn't quite shake their grip on me at the time.

But the Holy Spirit reminded me about what Jesus taught in Matthew 11:28 when He said, "Come to me all you who are weary and burdened, and I will give you rest. Take my yoke upon you and learn from me, for I am gentle and humble in heart, and you will find rest for your souls. For my yoke is easy and my burden is light."

Oh, if it were that easy! How could I release it all? What was the trick to letting go of my troubles and never picking them up again?

There was no trick; it was simple faith. I should have listened more closely to Jesus and taken Him up on His offer. He made very plain what I had to do. He extended one of His most sensitive invitations. He used soothing, comforting words such as *gentle*, *humble*, *easy*, and *light*. And that invitation is extended to all of us. He beckons us to Him and invites us to release all that concerns us into His hands. He is like a loving friend who has learned of our problems and offers to help. He tells us to let go and to let Him take over. I thought that I had done that. I thought that I had released it all. But I hadn't. Trouble was ever present before me, and it came with a disturbing amount of fear.

Unable to give my burdens to Jesus, I finally asked Him to take them away. "Please lift them from my shoulders," I asked. Depending on your struggle, you might not find it easy to take your problems to the Lord and leave them there, either. You might feel trapped, caged in by circumstances that you can no longer control. That's okay. We've all been there. I've witnessed God's limitless grace and received His countless blessings; yet, I still find myself worrying at times. As a new parent, I've found that it's virtually impossible *not* to worry about my child. Experienced parents have told me that I've only just begun to fret. Concern for our children starts the day we know they're in our wombs, and it never stops.

But Jesus reassures us that we don't have to worry. You'd think that His Word would be enough, right? After all, Our Savior said it. Who else needs to convince us beyond Him? My aunt tried when she told me, "If you're gonna pray, then don't worry. If you're gonna worry, then don't pray." She was right. So when I found myself beginning to worry, I began to pray. Prayer is an excellent replacement for worry. It fortifies us.

Another worry repellent is always to remember God's love for us. Until you weigh the magnitude of His awesome adoration, you tend to take it for granted, and you don't consider how colossal it is. Its vastness is beyond our purview of understanding. So we tend to forget the power of God's love when we're in trouble. I found it hard to feel His love for me when fear was stomping on me. God's love is the greatest of all truths. And no matter how daunting the dilemma before us might seem, He is closest to us then because He knows that we most need Him at that moment. He hears our prayers. He knows our sorrow. He feels our every ache and deep-seated pain. He laments with us. And because He does, He gives us a Comforter to console us.

If you are on a battlefield right now, have an earnest conversation with God. Share your greatest fears and concerns. Talk to Him as any child would to a father whom he knows can and will help him. He views us as His children, and He wants to hear from us. He wants to be in our lives. He wants us to depend on Him. And He wants to bless us with the desires of our hearts.

A meditation technique that worked for me during my time of trial was this: I envisioned myself seated at God's feet or with my head pressed against His chest. I imagined His arm around my shoulders or His right hand on top of my bowed head. I told Him all about my troubles. I held nothing back. I felt a release as I laid it all out for Him. Then I blessed the Lord for His goodness and for listening to me. I thanked Him for the fullness of my life and let Him know that I was ready to receive the blessings that He had set aside for me. I tried to look beyond my present circumstances and imagine the victory that lay ahead. Then I listened quietly for His response.

I learned that technique only after many nights of fighting. Before I learned to use it, I lay in the hospital for many days without realizing fully just how dire my situation was. Although I knew that I was in a critical situation (trust me, everyone said it over and over again), I still held out hope in the Lord. Although I felt helpless, I never felt hopeless. I know now that my survival wasn't because I had such great faith; it was the sustenance of God's grace.

When the neonatologist spoke, my spirit kept saying, *I know what your statistics show, but I know what my God can do—and He has never failed me.* Many people might think that failure comes with loss and death. For example, when we pray that a loved one's life be spared and yet they die, or when we pray that we reach a particular goal of ours but it doesn't happen, has God failed us? I have come to believe that although I've prayed earnestly for some things and did not receive them (e.g., that my mother would live when she was critically ill and my daily prayer that my family be kept safe although my brother died at the age of 46), I don't believe that God failed me.

As was mentioned earlier, our prayers are most successful when they are in line with God's will. We don't always know what's best for us or our loved ones; therefore, we *all* have chosen poorly and suffered the consequences. God permits these failings as lessons to us because He is a God of choice, and He allows us to choose. But on some occasions He, as any good parent would do, asserts His authority and says, "It is my will that life goes this way. . . ." We don't give our kids everything they want, and neither does the Lord.

I asked that my mother be spared, and He did spare her for two more weeks before she passed away. All of us who were out of town got a chance to see her. But had she lived beyond that, she would have suffered greatly from the effects of diabetes. In fact, she had already suffered greatly. She had three amputations and probably would have had to endure another, in addition to dialysis. Her eyesight was failing, with the real possibility of blindness on the horizon. She would have been homebound, bedridden, and in need of round-the-clock care. This person was not the jovial, robust woman I'd known. She had been relegated to a sickly, diseased body that was ready to quit.

And although I pray for my family's safety every day, I know realistically that we must all die someday. So I ask the Lord that He not allow any of my family members to die in their sins without developing a meaningful relationship with Jesus, their Savior. I pray for their salvation. And from the kind words that many people were eager to speak on my brother's behalf at his funeral, my prayers were answered. He apparently exhibited the behavior of one who knew the Lord and was fighting to live accordingly; therefore, his death was not a result of God's failure to honor the petitions I had requested. Rather, it was a testament that God answers the depths of our prayers—those words that go unspoken by us and those thoughts that even we have not brainstormed critically enough to weigh all of the outcomes. Our requests are often superficial, but God's answers are deep and effectual.

So I listened to the pessimistic comments of the doctor, and my husband and I asked questions. We were hopeful, yet realistic. If the baby did not survive, we asked about social services that could help us through the grief process and even funeral arrangements. We weren't sure if a funeral was appropriate for one so small. It was all too strange to consider.

Then began the many days of watching a fetal monitor. Two belts were strapped around my tummy, one to track my contractions and the other to monitor the baby's heart rate. Over the next several days and weeks, the resulting information became the deciding factor for whether to deliver the baby. The biggest concerns to the doctors were the possibility of infection or my going into labor. If infection occurred, they would deliver the baby immediately at the risk of losing him to save me. They thought that I could get pregnant again and have another baby if this one did not survive. They wanted to spare my life, thereby allowing me a chance at future attempts. So they put me on intravenous antibiotics over the first three or four days to prevent infection. I had to stay in bed flat on my back and sometimes in a position that practically had me standing on my head! Have you tried to eat that way? It's not a very appetizing position.

Every day I battled fear. And I think that I handled it pretty well in the daylight. But when night fell, it turned into unadulterated terror. I hated to see dusk descend on the day although each day that I completed was a blessing. Fear pushed me on the shoulder and bullied me into a fight. The scenario usually went like this:

The monitor in my room was linked to the monitors at the nurses' station. The belts were around my stomach sometimes twenty or more hours a day. When the nurses saw the baby's heart rate take a steep dive, they scurried into my room wearing concerned looks. They told me that if it kept up, they would have to call the doctor. In my state of mind, I interpreted this comment as a threat. They studied with knitted brows the tape that was printed from the monitor. Occasionally, they contacted the on-call doctor. The rise and fall of the baby's heart rate happened often, several times each day and night, so this scenario occurred more times than I care to remember. The nurses offered great care, but their worry added to my already heightened sense of fear. I stayed on edge because *they* were often on edge.

Nearly twenty nurses cared for me during the forty days that I was in the hospital. Every time a new one came on, I had to go through this scenario all over again. None of them ever got used to it although the doctors who were on call warned both them and me that this was to be expected and that there was no real need for alarm. They told us when we *should* become concerned—if the baby's heart rate dropped and stayed down for a long time or if I went into labor. But somehow the nurses still reacted the same. They were afraid, and their fear kept me edgy enough to cause more contractions. And the more contractions I had, the more the baby's heart rate dipped. And the nurses rushed in, and . . .

It seemed like an endless cycle. I hated that monitor. It kept everyone, including me, stressed. And I was attached to it almost twenty-four hours a day. By the time I delivered, my stomach was chafed and blistered from the belts.

On several occasions, I was given an injection that I came both to appreciate and to hate simultaneously. It was designed to stop contractions, and it did for a while. But its major side effect was an increased heart rate for me. I became jittery and shaky, and my heart pounded rapidly as though horses were galloping through my chest. It was a disturbing feeling. In addition, my back ached from lying in the same position for long periods. I was too afraid to move to get more comfortable because I'd have more contractions. So I'd try to lie still and deal with the pain. I felt tortured and imprisoned. When I had too many contractions while lying on my back, I lay on my left side. I spent probably 80 percent of my time on that one side day and night. I felt like the prophet Ezekiel, who lay on his side for 390 days eating one small meal cooked over manure.

In contrast to his predicament, I didn't have it as bad as it might have been, right? Nonetheless, I went through three beds during my nearly six weeks in the hospital. Every day was a struggle.

I called on the Lord in my angst. *What is going on Lord?* I wanted to know. *What am I to learn from this?* I surely didn't want to miss the lesson if I was going to go through this agony. I had never known a more humbling experience. Before facing this trouble, I thought that I was a rock and had unshakable faith. But the thought of losing this child turned that solid faith into Jell-O.® I managed to hold onto hope, but it was like trying to grip a greasy pipe. Nonetheless, I fought because I'd witnessed too many years of God's power to let go. And even during those terrifying days, He was on the front lines with me. There was no way that I could lose. It was too bad that I couldn't fully appreciate that notion at the time.

The Parable of the Persistent Widow (Luke 18:1–8)

1 Then Jesus told His disciples a parable to show them that they should always pray and not give up.

2 He said: "In a certain town there was a judge who neither feared God nor cared about men.

3 And there was a widow in that town who kept coming to him with the plea, 'Grant me justice against my adversary'.

4 For some time he refused. But finally he said to himself, 'Even though I don't fear God or care about men,

5 yet because this widow keeps bothering me, I will see that she gets justice, so that she won't eventually wear me out with her coming!'"

6 And the Lord said, "Listen to what the unjust judge says.

7 And will not God bring about justice for His chosen ones, who cry out to Him day and night? Will He keep putting them off?

8 I tell you, He will see that they get justice, and quickly. However, when the Son of Man comes, will He find faith on the earth?"

Chapter Two

The Contenders: Fear vs. Faith

S atan sent fear to torment me daily without fail. But it would retreat into a corner when visitors came, especially those who wielded prayer as a weapon. It was a coward in the face of faith. Many people who visited gathered around me, held hands with my husband and me, and prayed for a successful delivery and good health for the baby and me. What a comfort that was!

Strategy #2	Prepare an army for battle. Recruit prayer warriors.

This action brings us to Strategy #2: "Prepare an army for battle. Recruit prayer warriors." As is the case in any war, there is strength in numbers. Solicit the support of anyone who knows how to pray, and ask them to stand on the front lines with you. Gather as many of these warriors as you can.

Ask them to go forth boldly on your behalf, and ask God to cover you with His grace. Ask them to pray that you don't succumb to fear.

I yielded to fear many nights. When visitors were few, the war against it was on. It arose from its hiding place under the cover of darkness and taunted me. The monitors went haywire, my back ached, contractions started, and the baby's heart rate dipped. Then fear and frustration increased. And the tears flowed. Fear wore me down because I was alone, and no one was there to remind me of God's goodness and power. I'd have to remind myself. But it was hard to remember when everything in front of me was running amuck.

Many nights, I felt alone and weary, and I cried to the Lord for relief. I felt as though I couldn't go on. A great weight lay on my chest. A noose hung around my neck. I was afraid. Most frightening of all was the uncertainty about the future. I was tempted to believe Satan's lie that my baby would die, but I fought against the temptation. Hope prevailed. As the days progressed and my stomach grew with the baby, I was encouraged. But I was easily *discouraged* when I considered that I might have to let him go. I needed the Lord to show Himself, to comfort me, to enlighten me, and to fight for me. But He seemed to be silent. I fretted deeply after fear reminded me that God sometimes allowed babies to die.

In my desperation for some direction, I begged God to let me hear His audible voice. I wouldn't have flinched if He'd spoken directly to me as He had to Abraham, Moses, David, or Isaiah. I needed to hear from Him badly. I needed to hear God say that everything was going to be all right. I appreciated friends and family saying it, but it didn't carry the same weight. Only the Most High could assure me. I read His Word and sought confirmation. Several Scriptures spoke to me, and soon I was comforted. But the Evil One was always hovering around, trying to convince me that what was before me was what was real. When my stomach balled up in a knot on one side and I was having a contraction, that was real. When the contractions came four times in an hour, that was the real concern. Every time I had to get a shot or when I went to the bathroom and blood issued, those were the real deal. When I had to get an IV for one reason or another again and again, reality was happening. Fear was pushy, and it kept shoving such "realities" in my face.

Before this trial, I thought that I could take whatever the Devil dished out and shrug it off. But he had groomed my nemesis fear to be quite an intimidating adversary. I was buckling under the pressure. *How could I be so weak?* I asked myself. Where is my faith in God? Hadn't He proven Himself to me countless times already? How many times in the past did money appear just in the nick of time when I didn't know where I'd get it? How many scary plane rides had He brought me through safely? How many times did He protect me against threats on my job that could have ended my employment? How many times has He spared my father's life? How many ways has He delivered my alcoholic brother and made him into someone totally new?

The evidence was before me. Why was I allowing myself to crumble? A healthy dose of guilt was tied to these questions. I couldn't help feeling that I was letting God down. Fortunately, He didn't see it that way.

What I discovered was that God doesn't expect us to be a wall of steel during our trials. It's OK to have our defenses weakened when we're fighting as long as we're still fighting. We let Him down when we give up and when we stop pressing on despite the obstacles. We press on by staying faithful, continuing to pray, always trusting in God only, and rejoicing in the face of fear. God wants us to give our battles to Him, not fight them alone. If we could contend with trials by ourselves, then why would we need Him? Our needs draw us closer to Him. Giving in is not giving up. Even Jesus had to turn to His Father throughout His walk on earth. Life wasn't easy for Him either, and He held miraculous power in His hands.

"During the days of Jesus' life on earth, He offered up prayers and petitions with loud cries and tears to the One who could save Him from death, and He was heard because of His reverent submission." (Hebrews 5:7)

Jesus understood my pain. He understands yours. He had suffered to the point of tears and felt distraught enough to cry out to the Lord God. And God answered Him. He also answered me, and He will answer you, too. But note that Jesus submitted to the Lord with reverence. Do you approach God in the same way, or do you go to Him as though He's on your level? We can become irreverent in our relationship with God, even cocky in how we handle Him. Have you tried humility? Have you fallen upon your knees and cried out to Him? We must hold God in the highest regard. We must exalt Him to the utmost. We must give Him respect and not take Him lightly or trust in Him halfheartedly. He is supreme.

You might feel weighed down by your problems, but if you can find it in your heart to rejoice, then do so. It will lift your spirits. It will lighten your load. Keep thanking God for the joy that will come when the struggle is over. Try it. You will find that as you speak words of gratitude, you will feel it in your heart, and your outlook on your situation will change. And perhaps even your situation will change. James tells us that we should consider it pure joy when we face trials because the testing of our faith develops perseverance (James 1:2–3). Perseverance is staying power. Staying power through your ordeal with the promise of a blessing to follow.

I earnestly believed that I would come out victorious at the end of this adversity, although I could not rejoice as James recommended. I was too downtrodden. I didn't learn how to celebrate in the midst until I'd gotten home. So I asked Jesus to rebuke the winds and the waves in my life as He did when He was with the disciples on the lake. I asked Him for the same three words that He had spoken then: "Peace be still" (Mark 4:35–41). And peace did come.

He quieted the storm late one night when the contractions wouldn't cease and the baby's heart rate would not stay steady. I had become mentally and physically drained and was unable to rest. But after I prayed, I experienced a calm as though I'd entered the eye of the storm. The contractions ceased, and my son's heart rate was as steady as a rock. I slept. Praise God!

The one Scripture that rang through my mind repeatedly was Matthew 18:19–20: Jesus said, "I tell you that if two of you on earth agree about anything you ask for, it will be done for you by My Father in heaven. For where two or three come together in My name, there am I with them."

I held God to His promise. Many people were praying on our behalf, and I knew that He would grant our request. He requires that only two or three gather in agreement. But hundreds of people had gathered and were praying for me. I was on prayer lists from coast to coast. Even a Louisiana prison ministry lifted us up. I believe that petitions were rising to heaven all day every day on our behalf. *Surely, God will keep His Word and grant all of those requests*, I thought. I wondered how people who had no support system, especially a spiritual support system, made it through such trying times. Prayer was all that I had left—but it was also all that I needed. I encourage you to try it for yourself. Implement Strategy #2, and gather your prayer warriors for battle. I am a witness that it works.

I was also led to Matthew 7:7–8, in which Jesus said, "Ask and it will be given to you, seek and you will find, knock and the door will be opened to you. For everyone who asks receives, he who seeks finds, and to him who knocks the door will be opened."

I did as I was told. I sought, I knocked, I asked, and I believed. Surely, blessings were on the way.

The Word of God continued to sustain me, and I indulged in it daily to increase my confidence. Reading it was like a spiritual workout. It caused me to exercise my faith, build my spiritual might, tone up my prayer life, and condition myself for obedience. The Bible tells us that the Word of God is living and active (Hebrews 4:12). It is. Every time I studied it, I was infused with hope and peace. It breathed new life into me. It reminded me that God is compassionate and merciful. He does not delight in our suffering. He will empower us with the tools that we need to fight and be victorious.

And this brings us to Strategy # 3: "Choose your weapons—the shield of faith and your sword which is the Word of God." These are the two

> **Strategy #3** Choose your weapons—the shield of faith and your sword which is the Word of God.

most powerful weapons against fear. The sword cuts at the heart of fear and kills it. Where faith abounds, little room exists for fear. I came to learn through all of this warfare that when I raised the shield of faith before me, the fiery arrows that fear shot at me fizzled at my feet. They were rendered useless, and fear was forced to retreat and regroup. You raise your shield of faith by flatly refusing to accept the lies of the enemy, no matter how threatening reality seems to be before you. Operate on your deep-seated trust in God that He is overseeing all that is taking place, and you are protected because you asked Him for protection.

Raise your sword against the enemy by opening your Bible and eagerly seeking out what it has to say regarding your circumstances. If you plan ahead, you can beat the enemy before he strikes by reading the Bible daily and learning God's will and warnings. Then, when the enemy chooses you as its next target and tries to mislead and weaken you, you will be prepared. You will know the truth for yourself, and the Word cannot be mangled. You can use it to cut to useless pieces the lies of your adversary. When the enemy approaches you as Satan did Jesus when He was in the desert weak and hungry (He had fasted for forty days), and quotes Scripture, you can do as Jesus did. Rebuke him immediately and tell him what the Scripture really says. He will be forced to retreat, and you can raise your sword in victory.

For this reason, God allows us to go through hardships and take all of the bumps and bruises. He wants to teach us how to remain standing when the war is over. If you've ever been around teenagers or had any of your own, you can understand the quandary of trying to teach them and yet letting them learn life's lessons on their own. Many teens think that they know what's best for them. They don't think that they can or will get hurt in the many situations of which we warn them, and they think that adults tend to overreact. As a parent or guardian, you might feel forced to step back at times and let life happen without your intervention when the teen refuses to heed your warnings. Life does happen, and the very things that you predicted would occur usually do. Your young person might come out of their scrape a little banged up, but they are definitely wiser and (hopefully) more disciplined.

This is what happens to all of us who are God's children. He metes out to us the lessons that will transform us. And it's good that He does. You know as well as I do that if any of us had any choice over the trials in our lives, we'd opt for the least painful experiences. As a result, we'd learn very little about faith, mercy, obedience to God, or the awesome power of His Holy Spirit. In fact, we'd probably not have much use for God at all. We wouldn't bear much fruit, and He would hardly be glorified. That's why God doesn't always step in immediately when we experience trouble. He is always with us through it all, but He might choose not to steer us away from a pitfall.

The trite thought that "bad things happen to good people" is a testament to God's being on standby. If He rescued us and protected all that we loved every time danger struck, then we would know no pain. We'd never have to call on Him to deliver us from it, and we would cast Him aside and seek Him only when we got into trouble. We wouldn't pray or praise Him, and we'd probably never acknowledge His blessings because we wouldn't have any sorrows to balance their sweetness. Now that my ordeal is over, I'm considering it a privilege to have been chosen to endure such woe. Like Paul, I felt special when I considered the privilege to suffer for Christ after all He's done for me. He chose me. Would I let Him down? As hard as the test was at the time, I just couldn't.

When life happens in a big way, the lessons are large, too. They seem insufferable, but when God steps aside to allow them to happen, rest assured that He does not walk away. He is right there waiting in the wings. And when all that's left is the remnants of the way life used to be, He emerges to help us pick up the scraps. I've seen those pieces come back together to reveal a life that was better than it was before.

What trial are you battling now? Is it physical illness, financial woes, marital problems, relationship discord, depression, addiction, grief, or spiritual weakness? Whatever your dilemma, God is aware of it. And however the story ends, He is there to come to your aid, to rescue you if necessary, and to show you His love.

Let me tell you of another discovery that I made as I stumbled through my war against fear. I found a treasure in 1 Samuel that addressed the Holy Spirit and power. First Samuel 10:6 reads, "The Spirit of the Lord will come upon you [Saul] *in power*, and you will prophesy with them; and you will be changed into a different person" (emphasis added). 1 Samuel 10:10 says, "When they arrived at Gibeah, a procession of prophets met him [Saul]; the Spirit of God came upon him *in power*, and he joined in their prophesying" (emphasis added). Then later in chapter 11, verse 6, the Bible says, "When Saul heard their words, the Spirit of God came upon him *in power*, and he burned with anger" (emphasis added).

Every time the Spirit of God came upon Saul, He came upon him *in power*. And He does the same for us. When the Holy Spirit comes upon us, He does not possess our bodies like a demon. But when He comes, He empowers us to act boldly and authoritatively upon the situation before us. His arrival changes us and gives us dominion and command over our enemies. The Devil takes our power away from us. The Holy Spirit gives us the power that we need to fight and win. I desired His power so that I could stand up in the war against me. I prayed for the Holy Spirit to come upon me. I had been weakened by events that seemed to change by the hour. I needed His power to help me to stand and not to waver. I did not want to taste defeat.

Fear got in my face and my head and told me that I would surely taste defeat. I'd get a mouthful. At times, I felt as though my toes were hanging over the edge of a cliff and at any moment someone would come up behind me and push me off. I was always teetering around the fringes and wondering if this was the day when I'd have to deliver. And if I did, what would the end bring?

Despite my daily renewal of spirit through prayer and God's promises in His Word, I sometimes felt too weak to pray. Some days, I couldn't say more than, "Lord help me." And that was enough because God knew my circumstance. He doesn't need a long, drawn-out prayer and lengthy explanations. Three words and a mustard seed of faith were enough to silence the war that was raging around me. And He promised in Romans 8:26–28 that He has already provided our help when we feel drained emotionally. That Scripture says, "In the same way, the Spirit helps us in our weakness. We do not know what we ought to pray for, but the Spirit Himself intercedes for us with groans that words cannot express. And He who searches our hearts knows the mind of the Spirit because the Spirit intercedes for the saints in accordance with God's will. And we know that in all things God works for the good of those who love Him, who have been called according to His purpose."

This is powerful Scripture. Read it again if it has not sent a rush of relief over you. The Holy Spirit has been given to us to pray on our behalf when we are too weak to pray for ourselves. How great the Lord is! He knows that we'll have skirmishes that will leave us feeling downtrodden and defeated. But He offers us One who will lift us up when we think that we've hit bottom.

Are you flat on your back because fear has knocked you out? Or worse yet, are you flat on your face because fear has stolen your courage? Call on the Holy Spirit to raise you up.

Do not think you are too sick, too sinful, too depressed, too afraid, or too unwise in the ways of the Lord for Him to make use of your talents or tribulations. He will arm you with all of the resources you need to carry out His plans because your struggle is useful to Him. It serves as a testament of His might and mercy. Fear is the major culprit that can stand in the way of your trusting God to the fullest and being able to overcome your affliction. It can prevent you from loving because you fear losing, from speaking about Him because you fear rejection, and from taking a leap of faith because you fear failing. It only stifles your growth and progress in God, thereby decreasing your efforts to bear good fruit in His Name. Rebuke fear. Resist it before it robs you of your confidence and joy. It will flee if it is challenged, and you will be set free. Sometimes freedom from fear is closer than you think.

On May 9, I had a very strange yet revealing dream about fear. I saw a very large, high bridge. It was intimidating to me because I am afraid of heights. I was afraid to travel on it, and fear almost prevented me from going ahead. I was riding in a car with a stranger although I didn't feel threatened by him. Nonetheless, I wanted to get away from him. A huge traffic jam had occurred on the bridge in both directions. I didn't want to get stuck on this imposing structure in a car, so I asked the person to stop and let me get out and walk. In spite of my fear, I trod up the bridge because it was the only way to my destination. At some point, I got far enough along the bridge to freeze; I couldn't go forward or backward. I couldn't continue up or down. I was on some type of stairway, and all I could do was hold onto the railings for dear life.

Directly in front of me was a woman on the landing. She was ominous and wouldn't let me pass. She was an obstacle to my moving forward. Other people were behind me, and they were growing impatient because I was too terrified to move. So they started throwing their backpacks over the railing and jumping down to the next flight. They were successful, but still I was too afraid to follow them. Somehow, I managed to convince the daunting woman in front of me to let me pass. She did, and I moved my legs enough to wobble forward and around her. When I got past her, I was much relieved to find that the way down wasn't nearly as far as I'd thought. It wasn't nearly as frightening or threatening either. I was actually very close to the bottom, only two flights to the end, and I was safe. Afterward, I felt foolish for being afraid.

I awoke the next morning and remembered the dream vividly. I pondered it and tried to understand it. It was odd but intriguing. After

46

much consideration, I interpreted it to mean that whatever I was feeling in the hospital at the time was not insurmountable. All I needed to do was move forward despite my fears. I was closer to the end than I knew, and it would be alright once I got there. I had asked God to speak to me, and now I believe that He had done so through this dream. I heard the message of 2 Corinthians 1:3, 4: "Praise be to the God and Father of our Lord Jesus Christ, the Father of compassion and the God of all comfort, who comforts us in all our troubles, so that we can comfort those in any trouble with the comfort we ourselves have received from God."

This lesson shows the purpose for this book. How good it is to know that with whatever you're struggling, you are not alone. Many other people have faced the same trials that you face and have survived. And all who come to the Lord in their distress will be comforted. Often, you will be comforted by the shared experiences of people like me who have gone through an ordeal and were obedient to the urging of the Lord.

I was encouraged by these messages of hope, but the haunting continued. Finally, one day I listened to God only and blocked out the taunts of fear. The Holy Spirit spoke to me with great conviction, and I felt a wave of satisfaction in His explanation. He said, "If God is taking you through this war to act as a witness for Him, how could He be glorified if it ended in tragedy?"

Aha! The flicker of hope within me burned a little brighter. I started to work it out in my mind. How could I go out and proclaim God as the One who can and will do all that we ask in faith if the outcome to my situation was death and failure? With God, there is no failure. But fear sat on my shoulder and whispered, "Bad things happen to good people all the time. Many people have lost loved ones, even babies. How can you be sure that God won't take your child, too?"

But the Lord stepped in and said to me, "You asked Me to help you share the gospel with others in a great way. You told Me that you wanted to be of greater service to Me than you had been. You wanted to share My goodness and grace everywhere you went. I am glorified through triumphs because that's primarily what the minds of the people in this world can handle. It is more difficult to teach them triumph in the midst of tragedy. Somehow, they can't always see the victory in what seems to be a loss. So I will spare your child. When you finish telling this story, your child will be evidence that I am the Lord who answers the prayers of the righteous. I do keep the promises that are written in My Word. If others believe as you have, they, too, can reap the same rewards, and I can be glorified before all men."

Then He reminded me about His love for me. Somehow I had lost sight of it through the torment and anguish. His Spirit spoke to my heart and helped me remember that God does not take pleasure in our grief. He loves us more than we could ever love Him.

We do not serve a heartless, insensitive God, although Satan will try to lead us to believe that we do. God's Word is overflowing with His compassion and mercy for us. In 2 Corinthians 12:9, Paul wrote about how the Lord answered him in his distress and reminded him that His grace is sufficient for all of us. Paul wrote that the Lord's power is made perfect in our weakness. So he decided that he would boast gladly about his weaknesses so that Christ's power would rest on him. Paul delighted in weaknesses, insults, hardships, persecutions, and difficulties. He believed that when he was weak, he was made strong through Christ. What a wonderful freedom to allow ourselves to be weak and let Christ take over.

I wish now that I had realized the fullness of God's grace when I was being pounded in my fight with fear. When I should have been weak, I felt as though I was giving up. Fortunately, God knew my heart. He knew that I believed He could do all things. And even when I sat on the edge of fear, He knew that I was fighting to stay strong, positive, and faithful. For Him, I didn't want to give anything less of myself. I had erroneously equated surrendering with a lack of faith. As a result, I suffered needlessly.

God knows our frailties as humans. After all, He designed us. He wouldn't expect us to be a rock during difficult times. *He* wants to be that rock *for* us. He wants us to depend on Him and come to Him when we are in need. He wants to bless us so that *He* might be glorified. Through our blessings and testimonies, others can come to trust God, too.

I wish that I could have embraced His mercy more abundantly when I was struggling. I could have decreased my burdens. I used loads of energy fighting negative thoughts. Satan sent demon after demon to chisel and dig away at my faith.

Then finally, May 14 rolled in and was a great day of celebration. It was the day for which all of the medical staff had been waiting since the day my water broke. I had reached the twenty-eighth week of pregnancy. Hallelujah! The doctors thought that whenever I delivered after this time, the baby would be able to survive with fewer complications. Everyone came into my room that day saying, "It's week twenty-eight! It's week twenty-eight!"

My pastor had been visiting and keeping a tally. He and my congregation, along with family and friends, prayed for that twenty-eighth week. God heard and answered everyone's prayers. We had made it! Everyone let out a collective sigh, but we all still waited anxiously, hoping to eke out as much time as we could.

More than Conquerors
(Romans 8:37–39)

37 No, in all these things we are more than conquerors through Him who loved us.

38 For I am convinced that neither death nor life, neither angels nor demons, neither the present nor the future, nor any powers,

39 neither height nor depth, nor anything else in all creation, will be able to separate us from the love of God that is in Christ Jesus our Lord.

Chapter Three

The Duel in the Desert

uring my battle, I kept a journal with the intention of one day going back and reading the details to encourage myself. I also wanted something to give to my son when he got older. I want him to know how precious his life is and that it's not to be wasted. I want him to know how blessed he is. As I read some of my journal entries while I was working on this book, a lump rose in my throat. I had forgotten the details. Thank God for giving us short memories about bad times. The passage of time does soothe those old wounds. I will always remember that it was the worst experience of my life. But it wasn't until I reread the details that I could see God's hand at work against Satan's handiwork. The devil was busy, but God was busier. The entries were enlightening and uplifting. I sounded stronger on paper than I remembered myself being.

As I sparred with fear back then, I thought that the Lord was being silent. In retrospect, I now realize that He was in my corner of the ring coaching me, encouraging me, leading me to victory. He answered my prayers daily. But I took His answers for granted. I was so busy looking for the end of that trauma that I was blind to the successes along the way. I needed to get to twenty-eight weeks for my baby's best chance at a life with fewer complications. And I wanted week twenty-eight *immediately*. I missed the profound blessing that came at the end of every single day when God said, "Okay. You're a day closer." I couldn't hear Him. I had turned a deaf ear to my blessings but was keenly attuned to fear's threats. So I pleaded for help when help was already being given.

Each day that a visitor came by and talked to me; prayed with me; and prayed for my son, my husband, and me was a show of God's love. He sent His love with every person who walked through the door with a prayer on their hearts. But I didn't recognize it. Fear was hanging around my bed in the midnight hour, trying to convince me that God didn't love me. He had abandoned me when I needed Him most. But I learned to put up my shield of faith against his hateful lies. My faith told me that God would never abandon me although I was deaf to His responses.

I closed my eyes and meditated. I listened intently for His leading. But apparently there was some interference because the only thing I heard was silence. Only fear spoke loudly in my head while my body did all sorts of scary things that I couldn't control. I wanted God to make those things stop. I wanted the fluid to accumulate again. I wanted to go home and complete this pregnancy with no more drama.

But that wouldn't happen. I had to take this journey no matter how long or how uncertain it might be. I had to go forward blindly. I had to function on faith. It was the most sincere walk by faith that I'd ever taken. I could not see a minute ahead of me. Anything could have happened at any moment. No one could hazard a guess as to what would occur from one hour to the next. When would I go? Now? Would the baby be all right? Who knew? Only God. Faith was all I had–and it was enough.

However, fear was ever present. It was dark, mournful, threatening, and evil. The following entries from my journal indicate how I wrestled against its wickedness. Sometimes it had me pinned against the mat. But I would not stay down for the count.

The Duel in the Desert

May 3, Day 20 (3 weeks hospitalized)

I wrestled with Satan all night and this morning. I couldn't stop the fear or the tears. Even though my mind was screaming, "God is in control," my uterus was contracting and out of control. I had to get two shots yesterday. I feared I was going into labor. The baby is only 1lb., 12 oz. I really don't want to deliver him now. But it's not my call. Dr. Laffitte and Rene, the nurse, both prayed with me this morning when they saw my distress. I thought that was special. He told me to be weak so God could be strong in me. He's right. I must let go and surrender completely. I thought I had. But I guess I've picked up my burden again. It's hard to surrender and stay positive. It's like a contradiction. They seem to be impossible to do at the same time. I feel like I'm giving up on God when I surrender. But I'll learn how. After all, I still have great faith in Him. And if I should deliver soon, so let His will be done.

May 19, Day 37

O Lord, our Lord, how majestic is Your Name in all the earth! This has been the most trying week yet. We are inches from week 29 and yet it seems so far away. The physical symptoms from my body are causing my hope to waver at ever seeing 34 weeks completed. Yet I know I asked the Lord for them. Am I losing faith by giving in and saying, "Oh well, maybe I won't make it that far?" I don't doubt what the Lord can do. But I am in dire need of encouragement. Today, though, I feel the Spirit comforting me. They removed the ITC from my wrist, so I have more freedom to move about. I may be able to go outside for a little while, the first time in five and a half weeks. The numerous contractions I felt all yesterday evening have subsided, and the baby isn't taking huge dips anymore. Praise God. Every day brings something different. But it seems that every time I decide to give up and accept whatever will happen, then things get much better. Is that what God wants from me? Total surrender? I thought

I had. But perhaps I continue to pick up this battle unwittingly. All I'm really trying to do is have faith. I don't want to appear to doubt God by giving up. Lord, make this clear to me. How do I maintain my faith in Your will for this situation and surrender at the same time?

Strategy #4 Establish a strategy against the enemy.

I had many questions but no plan for how to maintain the upper hand in this war. It was a tug-of-war. First I'd prevail, then fear would get the edge. Then the victory would be back in my favor, but fear would trip me up again. So I had to implement Strategy #4: "Establish a strategy against the enemy."

No goal can be accomplished unless a strategy is in place with tactics to get you to the end. I didn't have a plan, a goal, a strategy, or tactics, so I was flying by the seat of my pants. As a result, I wavered a lot.

In any aspect of your life, you should have in place a plan for times when trouble comes calling. Otherwise, you will naively be caught off guard as I was. The enemy doesn't come at you when you're looking for him; he waits until you are vulnerable. Remember the prank when life goes, "Boo!"? Our opponent uses the element of surprise effectively to cripple us in the beginning. We must always be dressed and equipped appropriately, ready for any attack and ready to wage war when challenged. Fear and I were already exchanging blows by the time I realized that I didn't have a plan in place. So the battle raged, and sometimes fear was beating me.

Fear deftly stirred up enough confusion to lead me to believe that I was fighting to be faithful. But what I was really fighting was fear itself. I had faith that God would see me through this, but I was fearful of the route that He would take in getting me there. Would I be one of those people who would share her story by saying, "Although my son didn't make it, God gave me the strength to make it through"? I had not lost faith, but it was tipping from one side to the other like the scales of Justice. Faith would increase and fear would decrease. But then something scary would happen, and fear would increase while faith decreased. Faith and fear cannot—and should not—be balanced. Between these two, it's all or nothing, one or the other. Besides, fear will not allow you to have faith—not when fear is evil and is trying to break you.

When fear becomes evil, it confuses us about what we know is true. We think too much. We listen to the wrong people. We try to second guess God. We try to predict the outcome when all we need to do is wait on the Lord and trust that He's taken action. A revelation for me was that my fear of surrendering to God in this ordeal led me (under the guise of thinking that I was giving up on Him) to resist His urgings. His Spirit kept leading me to total surrender, but I fought it. As I noted in my journal entry, things got better once I capitulated. I believe now that if I hadn't resisted raising the white flag of unconditional surrender, I would not have had to struggle as much as I did. I would have been confident through faith that God was at work to give me the best possible outcome. I believe now that I struggled needlessly. But it wasn't totally in vain. When I walk through a valley again, fear will shudder in my wake.

I've learned that fear is evil when it steals our peace of mind. When we lose sleep and are haggard, we have given fear control. When we are anxious and agitated every day, we have yielded to fear. When we should be making a move forward but our feet are cemented to a safe spot, we have given our power to fear. When courage eludes us and our life dreams get lost under a pile of "what ifs," then fear has won. It is working against us and has asserted its enmity undaunted.

Examine your own life. Are you facing trouble on your job and are lost about how to overcome it? Is there tension and estrangement between you and your spouse, children, in-laws, friends, etc.? Are you contemplating suicide because life has become unbearable? Stop. Give up on destructive thinking. Don't hold on to any part of it. Peter urges us in 1 Peter 5:7 to cast all of our anxiety on God because He cares for us. It is not our burden to bear.

One great day, after I had fought this raging battle for more than a month, the Lord God brought all of my suffering to an end. He had taken me past the twenty-eight-week mark that the doctors and I desired. Two days shy of my making the twenty-ninth week, the contractions became much more intense, and the medication to stop them no longer worked. It was time to have the baby. I held on to 1 Peter 5:7, and I did cast all of my cares on the Lord. Everything was in His hands anyway. I didn't have any control. No one did. And I felt an odd sense of relief once I made that decision.

At 9:15 P.M. on May 19, my son, Justice Emile Parker, was delivered, and the medical staff was shocked by how healthy he was. He was 2 lbs., 9 oz., bigger than we'd seen on the ultrasound three days earlier. The biggest surprise was that he didn't require oxygen, and he showed no signs of any other problems. Everyone was in awe and extremely excited. By this time, the medical staff was deeply involved in the outcome of the pregnancy. They were as relieved as I was. I was grateful and overcome by God's blessing of my son. Hallelujah! It was over—at least this part.

Now the devil was really miffed. God had given me the victory, but He still had more to show me. This would be an enormous life lesson. And Satan saw this as another opportunity to inflict fear worse than he had before. I had wrangled with trepidation for nearly forty days and had finally triumphed by the power of the Lord and His Comforter, the Holy Spirit. Like Noah who had to spend forty long days in a storm, I was thrilled with new hope once my storm was over and I discovered "dry land." But that land was arid, barren, and desolate. Like Jesus, I would have to spend forty more days in the desert to be tempted by Satan. My battle was only half over.

In the beginning, my desert experience would prove more difficult than had been my first forty days on the front line. I didn't think that life could get much worse. And it wasn't; it only *seemed* that way because

I had no reprieve from fear. But God started firing off rounds of revelations, and I could hardly grasp them all. As the days passed, God began revealing Himself, peeling away layers that I had not known before. He no longer seemed far away. In fact, He was as close to me as He'd always been. He began showing me the reasons why I had to endure what I did during the first forty days. He strengthened me and renewed my hope in Him during this time.

As had happened to Jesus after His time in the desert, when angels came to minister to Him, I felt the Holy Spirit nearby ministering to me after my horrendous time at war. I felt His presence when my gait turned from ambling to trudging. He pushed me forward and consoled me. When my heart began to sag in my chest, a spring of warmth and contentment rose up and pushed the heaviness aside. When my nerves were raw from facing another day of waiting and uncertainty, He soothed me with the reminder that we had made it through the first rough period *triumphantly*.

But now more fear was to come. I had to leave my baby in the Neonatal Intensive Care Unit, or NICU. The feeling of separation was the worst part. In the beginning, I sometimes wasn't allowed to hold him. It was agonizing to watch my child through the glass of the incubator and not be able to embrace him. I then came to understand why Jesus agonized on the Mount of Olives the night before Judas betrayed Him. He knew that taking on the sins of the world would cause separation between Him and His Father. The thought was devastating to Him. When I realized that fact, I knew that He understood my grief. He, too, had experienced the emptiness of separation, and it hurt worse than any physical pain. I felt isolated, hollow, and alienated. No one but the Lord could understand my despair. So I prayed to Him just as Jesus did when He was distraught. Luke tells the story poignantly in his gospel account.

Jesus went out as usual to the Mount of Olives, and His disciples followed Him. On reaching the place, He said to them, "Pray that you will not fall into temptation." He withdrew about a stone's throw beyond them, knelt down and prayed. "Father, if You are willing, take this cup from me; yet not My will, but Yours be done." An angel from heaven appeared to Him and strengthened Him. And being in anguish, He prayed more earnestly, and His sweat was like drops of blood falling to the ground. When He rose from prayer and went back to the disciples, He found them asleep, exhausted from sorrow. "Why are you sleeping?" He asked them. "Get up and pray so that you will not fall into temptation." (Luke 22:39–46)

Can't you feel His sorrow? He prayed until His body poured sweat and the droplets resembled blood. I can see His damp hair, the sweat dripping from its ends, His clothes stuck to His body from the perspiration, and His body drained from crying out to the Lord. He was breathing heavily. When He pushed Himself up from His knees, He felt as though He were already carrying a heavy cross upon His shoulders. His steps were labored as He trudged to find His disciples. Notice that an angel from heaven came to bolster Him.

We have that same resource. He's called the Holy Spirit. Jesus left Him here for us so that when we, too, find ourselves in situations in which nothing but prayer will do, we can find solace through His Spirit.

I also prayed more earnestly when I was in anguish. It was all I could do. Nobody but the Lord could strengthen me in my fragile situation. No doctor, no friend, and not my husband. Not even I could provide the necessary strength. Only God could do that. My husband and I kept our child covered in prayer day and night, and I solicited the prayers of others. Just because he had been delivered safely didn't mean that it was time to stop praying. He still had a long way to go, and so did I. Many scary moments lay ahead, and I was not prepared for them. The more dire a situation, the more earnestly we should pray. We must follow the example that Jesus set for us.

Once again, fear tried to disrupt my peace. I could not rejoice fully in the victory that God had given me because it was marred by the potential dangers ahead. Fear is a thief and will steal your joy. I regret that I ever allowed it to cast a shadow over my time of celebration. Fear was vicious the second time around, showing me repeatedly how close to death my child was.

Because he was born prematurely, my son was subject to something called A & B episodes. A, for apnea, meant that he sometimes stopped breathing. B, for bradycardia, meant that his heart rate often dropped suddenly. Because he was supposed to be practice breathing *in utero*, and I was supposed to be breathing for him, he sometimes forgot to breathe on his own. Apparently, this condition is common among such young babies, but it was nothing common to me. What mother can take her child's cessation in breathing lightly? He was in an incubator attached to more wires and monitors than I could stand to see. The alarms seemed to go off constantly (along with those of all of the other babies in the NICU, which is a very noisy place).

The way he looked was scary, too. He was frail and wrinkled. His breathing looked exaggerated because he had no body fat. His ribs were readily visible beneath his thin skin. The nurses wouldn't let me hold him at first, and that restriction was agonizing, but it was also frightening to consider holding him because he was so tiny. I thought that I might break him. I could pick him up with one hand like a can of vegetables, but a can of vegetables probably would feel heavier. A feeding tube was inserted down his throat, undoubtedly irritating him, and he eventually kept pulling it out. He had an IV in his tiny wrist. And leads were attached to his chest to monitor his breathing, heart rate, and temperature. Because preemies have no body fat, their body temperatures drop quickly. They must be kept warm in an incubator, so we couldn't keep him out very long when they did allow us to hold him.

Because he was so thin, when he stopped breathing, it took mere seconds for him to turn blue. Although it required only a gentle stroke on his bottom or his back to get him breathing again, I cringed every time it happened. And for my son it happened often. They gave him medication for it, but only time would rectify this problem. He would simply have to outgrow it, and he was still a long way from his due date.

On some days, however, the gentle stimulation would not work either. The nurses rubbed him, patted him, and even pinched him, but he did not respond. He turned dark gray, as if he were dead. The monitors squealed his distress. Then the nurses had to give him whiffs of oxygen immediately. Almost instantly, his heart rate accelerated again. These times were the most frightful moments of all for my husband and me. On two occasions, Justice went limp in my husband's arms. He passed out and became like a rag doll. Although my husband is a doctor, these episodes unnerved him. Once again, the nurses gave Justice oxygen to revive him. The special times we longed for in holding him became stressful. We'd put him back in his incubator immediately and watch him nervously through the glass. Fear danced around in front of us and tormented us with the fragility of our son's life. And it would be a while before these new trials would be over.

I approached every visit with trepidation. It made my efforts to go see Justice a strain. I found the NICU environment depressing. My depression was magnified by the post-partum blues that I was also feeling. Although I hated going to the NICU, I couldn't stay away. My child was there. I *had* to go—both day and night. The nights were the worse because eventually I had to leave the hospital. Then I had to suffer through long, excruciating hours at home until I could go back and see him again the next day. I felt fragmented without him, as though parts of me were missing. I ached for him. And then fear visited me in my bedroom at home and told me that while I was away, all kinds of awful things were happening to him. In essence, it was true. I usually received some negative news about him the following day.

The scariest moments were facing those closed doors of the NICU and wondering what awaited me on the other side. Would it be bad news? Would there be some kind of setback? Would he be stalled and not progress? I didn't want to hear anything that suggested that we would face a longer period of separation. My husband and I were always eager to get to our son, but facing those doors sent ripples of anxiety through us. We longed for the day when we'd be where some of the other parents were whose children were almost out of the NICU.

But who were we to complain? Some parents were struggling worse than us. I met a wonderful woman whose daughter had been in the NICU for nearly six months when Justice got there. After learning of her baby's critical condition, I kept them in prayer. Despite the prayers, the child died. Fear told me that the same thing could happen to Justice. And that baby wasn't the only critical one. Another woman's daughter had been on the ventilator from the day she was born in March. They had little hope that the child would ever come off. The last I heard, she was being moved to the pediatric ICU (PICU) in another city because she was still on the ventilator. By then, she was almost a year old, and her poor mother had never taken her home.

Oh, how my heart goes out to that family. How scared do you think those parents are? It's like sitting around waiting for your baby to die. Each grueling day is spent watching your child suffer. I pray for them even today. The thought of what they must be going through is torturous, and I can't begin to know their pain and exhaustion. I still continue to pray for every baby in every NICU all over the world. Please do the same.

When fear kept presenting these sorrowful stories to me, I prayed to keep from worrying. I prayed to keep from crying. I prayed to gain strength. It helped. I continued living from day to day, wondering what each new day would bring. Although I was afraid to move forward, I wanted to do so. I wanted my child to get to the point when he would finally be out of that place. I had had enough of hospitals! But I knew that we had a long road ahead of us. The NICU staff told me so. I sighed deeply and trod ahead just as Jesus had done.

Day in and day out, I visited Justice in the NICU and watched him make slow progress toward developing and growing to full-term status. He had arrived in this world three months ahead of schedule, and the staff told me to expect him to get out of the NICU around his due date. I couldn't bear the thought, so I didn't think about it. I prayed to God to bless him by allowing him to develop quickly and be home sooner. I created a schedule that helped me get that prayer answered. Here's what I did.

First, I read Scripture, figuratively eating the Word of God for spiritual nourishment. I revisited the gospel of Luke to reacquaint myself with the awesome deeds of Jesus Christ. I knew that He was a healer, and I wanted to read again about the miracles He'd performed in the lives of those who needed them. Most of His miracles were for those who needed physical healings.

Second, I got on my knees and prayed to God. I laid out in my mind and heart every thought as I spoke to Him—sometimes aloud. I went to Him just as I would have gone to my earthly father if he could have fixed my situation. I confessed my fears, my weaknesses, my frustrations, and my anguish and asked Him to provide His Comforter to me. His Holy Spirit came upon me in power, and the feelings of depression and hopelessness soon faded away. I gained strength and faced the day with decreasing trepidation.

Third, I took the time to lift my hands and praise the Lord for all of the blessings I'd received. In the midst of it all, I sometimes had a hard time seeing them, but God was already showering down His greatness upon me. My prayers were being answered even before I got off my knees because I would go into the NICU preparing for the worse. Often, the news would not be too bad, but the people who delivered it did so in such a way that it frightened me. I asked the Lord to take away anything that could be delivered as threatening. If nothing was wrong, then they wouldn't have anything to report. He did just that.

Nonetheless, I couldn't help approaching the NICU doors like a death-row inmate walking to the electric chair. My heart would race and then plummet to the pit of my stomach. Walking across the threshold, I felt as though someone had dropped a yoke around my neck. The only thing that gave me relief was the soothing arm of the Holy Spirit as He nudged me inside and sat with me as I held my son. Then I would feel as though a load had been lifted. God was showing Himself to me through the miracles that He was working in my child. The love that I felt for my son was the love that I knew the Lord felt for me. But His love was far greater than mine. His love was pure, unconditional, and infinite. I'd never known such love before. Oh, how I cherished those moments with Justice. And so did my husband.

God cherishes those same kinds of moments with us. He wants to hold us in His arms and console us. He wants to give us everything that we need because we are essentially helpless and can do nothing without Him. All He wants is our love in return and for us to accept His Son as our Savior. He wants us to love one another, too. It should be easy to do, yet we make our lives difficult by being disobedient.

Fear interrupted those special moments and told me of two more babies who had passed away in the NICU. I watched one mother wheeled out still in her hospital gown. Her face was buried in her hands, and she was sobbing. Two family members walked alongside her with faces sagging. The hospital social worker, who brought up the rear of that sad procession, later explained to me that the woman's baby had passed away only hours after her birth.

On another occasion, I walked out of the NICU to see a gathering of no less than thirty people outside its doors in a small waiting area. They were all hugging each other and wiping away tears. *This can't be good,* I thought. As I continued down the corridor, I heard a gentleman from the group talking on his cell phone away from the crowd. He was explaining to someone that the baby had lived only eighteen hours before it died. At the elevator, I ran into a trio hurrying to this crowd with looks of hope and a big pink bear boasting a ribbon that read, "It's a girl." What they were about to learn seemed cruel. Fear told me that my child could easily face the same fate. But God kept showing me His favor. He honored my prayers and the prayers of everyone who prayed with me by granting us what we requested. God is faithful to His Word.

Although this book is about triumph in the midst of fear, I would be remiss if I didn't take the opportunity to address those people who don't think that God has favored them. Parents who have lost children, people who are facing the possibility of death (whether their own or that of a loved one) from a terminal illness, people whose families are broken apart for whatever reason, and people who are abused, addicted, and anxious. "Where is your justice, God?" you might be asking. I mention it throughout the book, but I will say again that your condition, the status of your life, and the outcome of your problems rest in your relationship with God.

He deals with us individually concerning what He wants from us and for us. I might experience hardship in a different area of my life than you do. You might prevail victoriously through what was a tragedy for me. The simple fact of life is that we will *all* struggle through *something*. We will all face some circumstance that will yank at our hearts and cause us much grief. We will all shed tears of sadness and come to know the pains of a broken heart.

But if we stand by God through it all, He will provide His Comforter to us. He will not leave us to go it alone. And *through* it we will discover a deeper insight into life and our relationship with Him—an insight that will allow us to comfort someone else, teach someone else, help someone else, or prepare us for a greater responsibility to God if we dare accept it. If we choose not to become bitter and angry with God when we face such terrible times, so bitter and angry that it is protracted and weakens our relationship with Him, then He will bless us for holding on and holding out. We *will* find joy again. We will want to shout praises unto Him because blessings beyond what we could imagine will come our way. The pain will decrease, and the victory will once again be ours. It's hard to see that fact at first, but it does happen.

As the days passed and I continued to pray and praise; Justice progressed by leaps and bounds. This is the success of Strategy #5: "Declare war on the enemy, and don't stop fighting until it is defeated." With an army of prayer warriors surrounding me and the Holy Spirit inside me,

> **Strategy #5** Declare war on the enemy, and don't stop fighting until it is defeated.

God answered our passionate pleas. I was tired of being scared, and it was time to declare war on my enemy. After all, war had already been declared on me. I refused to back down, and the only way to rid myself of this nuisance was to keep on fighting until I had defeated it. I would not stop until I had beaten it.

The trips to the NICU got only slightly easier because the chasm between my son and me still existed. He was not in my care twenty-four hours a day, and I missed the bonding for which I'd longed while I was pregnant. I hardly knew this little guy. He had never been in our house, but I missed him as though he had been there and was taken away abruptly. It was an empty feeling to go home with everything looking much as we'd left it. He came so early that we hadn't had much time to prepare for him. It was as though we'd never had a baby. So I tried to busy myself with preparations for his homecoming. In the beginning, I was somewhat afraid to buy too much stuff. I wasn't sure that he'd make it. There again, fear produced doubt and compromised my faith. The tug-of-war continued.

I allowed the Lord to minister to me during the days in which the baby was hospitalized. I knew that I could learn significant lessons from this experience, so I asked God for wisdom. I took advantage of the time

> **Strategy #6** Attack the enemy where it is weak.

alone at home. With no other children in the house and my husband away at work most of the day, the Lord and I had plenty of time together. I didn't turn on the television or the radio. I listened for His words to be spoken to my heart. He led me to Strategy #6: "Attack the enemy where it is weak."

This strategy was crucial because it applied not only to me but also God would have me use it to aid another couple. In fear's effort to take another jab at my courage, it caused trouble with the baby who spent most of his NICU stay in the incubator next to my son's. The little boy's health issues were almost identical to those of my son. They almost seemed to play off one another. If Logan's heart rate dropped or he stopped breathing, my son would soon follow and vice versa. Their incremental weight gain was similar, and, like my son, Logan once refused to be stimulated and scared his parents when he turned dusky. But that wasn't the scariest thing to happen.

One night, something happened to Logan that we did not experience with Justice (thank God). It looked as though he would suffer a type of intestinal infection called necrotizing enterocolitis (NEC), which is usually devastating to preemies and can require surgery at its worst. It usually occurs after the first few tube feedings. My husband and I were visiting Justice and overheard the doctors' discussion at Logan's incubator. The parents were on their way, and I could only imagine what the long ride to the hospital must have been like for them. As my husband and I moved to allow room for the x-ray technician, my heart felt like a stone in my chest. As personally as I took their comments, they could just as easily have been talking about Justice. I was deeply saddened.

Finally, the parents arrived looking bewildered and concerned. Upon hearing the terrible news, the young mother was soon in tears. The doctors suggested trying the baby on antibiotics first. If he didn't respond, they would consider surgery in the morning. (Of course, this trauma would occur at night when things always seemed much scarier. But this would have been scary even in the daytime. This situation was serious.) When the doctors left, my husband suggested that we go to the couple immediately and offer to pray with them. We put Justice back inside his incubator (he was doing well enough at this time for us to hold him for a while), and we went over and asked them if we could pray with them. They only nodded, too hurt to speak.

They could not remove Logan from his incubator because he was too sick. He was limp and listless. The nurses had to start an IV for the antibiotics, and his formula feedings via a stomach tube would have to cease until he overcame the infection. He would also be fed by IV. This complication could delay his weight gain, which was one of the criteria for his getting out of the NICU. But he had bigger problems than low weight at the time.

My husband and I sandwiched the couple between us. We placed our hands on them and the incubator. They were able to touch their baby by slipping their hands into a slight opening in the incubator. I closed my eyes and prayed aloud for God's healing hands upon Logan. I asked Him to show His mercy and protect Logan against any disease. I asked Him humbly to restore Logan's health and put him back on the road to progress. I prayed for the strengthening of the parents and for all of the other suffering babies in the NICU. After I had finished making all of our petitions in the healing name of Jesus, we hugged the couple and offered words of encouragement. The young mother could not stop crying. Then we departed.

On the drive home, I continued to pray earnestly for Logan as if he were my own baby. I couldn't stop myself from praying. The Spirit seemed to be urging me on, so I remained obedient to Him. I prayed and prayed until I got home.

The next day, the answer was waiting for us. As soon as we walked to Justice's incubator, the couple was waiting. Smiles lit up their faces. They had good news. Logan had recovered in a big way overnight. The nurses couldn't stop talking about the immediate about face he'd taken. He was alert, his color was better, and, best of all, he would need no surgery. Hallelujah! The parents thanked us vigorously for our prayers. All I could do was praise God. Even now, I thank Him for being a God who can, a God who does.

Our prayers weakened the enemy (Strategy #6). We attacked it with the power of prayer. Fear cannot stand up to the might of prayer. It is a potent weapon because it produces actions that are measurable, extraordinary, and undeniable. James 5:16 says that the prayers of the righteous are powerful and effective. In Ephesians, Paul gives accolades to "Him who is able to do immeasurably more than all we ask or imagine according to His power that is at work within us" (Eph. 3:20).

When I prayed, I didn't put any limits on God. I believed that He could do more than my finite thinking could ever imagine. So I asked Him to unleash His awesome healing power upon Logan, and I didn't doubt.

Jesus said that we could use His Name when making our requests. People love to name drop. Here's one name that really does get results, results that even the most powerful man on earth couldn't produce. Only God. Only Jesus. Only the Holy Spirit.

I believe that God rewards us for our obedience and our faith. Not long after that most frightening test, my husband and I were rewarded with exciting news of our own. We were told that we could prepare for our son's arrival home in about two weeks. That was the first definite news we'd heard since the day he'd entered, and we felt as though we were Power Ball winners. The end was at hand. We would be taking home the big prize. What a great feeling! Joy flooded my heart for the first time since I'd heard that he was doing well after delivery. I could feel God's blessings getting ready to shine down on us in even greater ways, and I began to praise Him for whatever was on the way.

On July 7, 2001, I dug a grave for fear and promptly buried it. I gathered up my little bundle of four pounds, seven ounces, and whisked him home. He had spent seven weeks in the NICU instead of twelve weeks. God brought him home to us early just as we'd asked Him to do. Fear could no longer hang its threats over my head. I was holding the evidence of God's might and power in my arms. How to care for one so small and needy was intimidating. But my peace was restored, my joy was renewed, and my faith was revived in the highest. I had waged war on fear and won.

> Strategy #7 Claim the victory and rejoice!

At this time, I implemented the final strategy, #7: "Claim the victory and rejoice!"

What more can I say? God is magnificent. His goodness is beyond description. As one who is a recipient of one of His miracles, I lift Him up before you and all mankind. No one can convince me that He did not bring my baby from the possibility of demise to full recovery. While medical personnel stood by and wrung their hands and delivered caution and doubt, God kept assuring me that this was how He showed up best. It was all in His plan—a plan that is simple enough for you to use, too.

In Chapter 5, I put together all of the steps of how to annihilate fear. Use these strategies in your own fight and declare the victory. No matter what you're going through, if you are afraid, apply these next tactics boldly. God never said that we shouldn't be afraid. He just said that we didn't *have* to be. Expect to win!

God's Love
(1 John 4:7–16)

7 Dear friends, let us love one another, for love comes from God. Everyone who loves has been born of God and knows God.

8 Whoever does not love does not know God, because God is love.

9 This is how God showed His love among us: He sent His one and only Son into the world that we might live through Him.

10 This is love: not that we loved God, but that He loved us and sent His Son as an atoning sacrifice for our sins.

11 Dear friends, since God so loved us, we also ought to love one another.

12 No one has ever seen God; but if we love one another, God lives in us and His love is made complete in us.

13 We know that we live in Him and He in us, because He has given us of His Spirit.

14 And we have seen and testify that the Father has sent His Son to be the Savior of the world.

15 If anyone acknowledges that Jesus is the Son of God, God lives in him and he in God.

16 And so we know and rely on the love God has for us. God is love. Whoever lives in love lives in God, and God in him.

Chapter Four

"Justice" Prevails

Jesus encourages us in Matthew 10:27 to tell everyone what He's done for us. He says, "What I tell you in the dark, speak in the daylight; what is whispered in your ear, proclaim from the roofs." So here it is. God is real. He is a miracle worker. He answers prayer. And He loves us. Out of His infinite love for us, He gave the life of His only Son. He gave me a son, too, and showed me a love like none that I could have imagined. My son, Justice, won against the enemy. My husband and I won against the enemy. Justice prevailed.

A name can incorporate voluminous meaning, and if we want our children to live up to them, we should choose their names carefully. I had chosen my son's name *before* my crisis. I was looking forward to his honoring its meaning fully when he became a man. I had no idea how prophetic it would be even before his birth. Who knew that we would be seeking justice in so many ways? And who knew that God would enjoy giving it (and him) to us in a way that only He could give? Psalm 11:7 affirms it: "For the Lord is righteous, He loves justice; upright men will see his face." He loves justice. He loves *Justice*. I'm grateful for His love. Hallelujah! I rejoice in His love.

In hindsight, if I had to experience that ordeal all over again, I would surely follow the strategies outlined in the next chapter. They have been proven effective against fear. They worked for me, and they can be successful for you, too. Do not add more suffering when the answers for avoiding some of the hardships have already been provided for you. My responsibility as a disciple of Christ is to "speak in the daylight" and "proclaim from the roofs" what the Lord has shown me and told me. Your responsibility as a disciple of Christ is to be obedient to the messages. A disciple is a "follower." If you consider yourself a follower of Christ—a Christian—then take heed.

Now that I've survived this war, I have to share with you the wisdom that I've gained. I hope that you will be encouraged. Life can be a real hypocrite sometimes. It'll embrace us and push us along with great success. It'll make us happy to be alive and want to count all of our blessings. It'll help us appreciate the trees, the birds, and the sun's warm rays. It'll tell us that we've made it and that greater things are on the horizon for us. But as quickly as we're rolling along, basking in the glow of all that glitters, life will stand on the brakes, throw us forward, bang our heads against the dashboard, and propel us into a reality that we're sure that we could do without.

Is that where you are right now? What worries you today? What ugly reality has presented itself to you and told you to deal with it? As I've mentioned, my situation is by no means unique. One in every ten children is born prematurely. Some of them come earlier than others. Some of them, like my beautiful Justice, go on to be as normal as any full-term baby. In fact, my niece was only 1 lb., 15 ozs. when she was born. She spent four months in the hospital. Today, she's a healthy twelve-year-old (although she has asthma). Others go on, but their quality of life is compromised. They are left with many complications, including blindness, breathing problems, and cerebral palsy. And some preemies never make it.

All of those babies' parents have stories to tell. I'm sure that they fought this battle in many different ways. I couldn't go on without acknowledging how I fought mine. What happened to me is a testament of how great God's power is. Any of us who have overcome should be shouting it from the rooftops because no miracle is common, no matter how many times it's been performed. Yes, many women have had miracle babies. Actually, every baby is a miracle. Having worked in the field of reproductive medicine for a decade, I'm amazed that the world is as populous as it is. When you consider that a woman has only about two to three days every month during which to conceive, and a host of things must be working in sync for that to happen successfully, it is a wonder that any woman gets pregnant at all. That's why life is truly a gift that should never be taken for granted or wasted. And when death comes calling even before the life has made its debut into the world as in my case, then we must seek a miracle. We have no other recourse. To come close to losing a life only to have God step in and make the situation right is nothing to cast aside as commonplace. He must be glorified.

Would I want to shout as loudly if I were the lady whose baby has been on a ventilator in the NICU for the past eleven months with no hope of bringing her home? Probably not. Who can celebrate when what seems like defeat is laughing in your face? But I would have to ask myself, *What lies beneath it all? Surely, this torture has not been for naught. God does not permit such actions just because it's my turn to be on sorrow's wagon. No. There is more.* I would search out His Spirit just as I did when I was going through my own trial. I would ask the following questions:

- "How should I view this trauma so that I do not allow grief to make me bitter?"

- "This event is very painful, Lord. What result is this agony supposed to yield?"

- "Is this a test, Lord, or a punishment?"

- "If it is a test, how do I pass? And what is my reward in the end?"

- "If it is a punishment, how do I yield to your discipline?"

- "How do I remain encouraged at a time like this?"

- "Why was this particular test chosen for me?"

- "Where is the triumph in this apparent defeat?"

- "What action, if any, must I take, Lord, to make it through?"

All of these questions have answers. God might reveal them to you immediately, over a period of time, many years from now, or in the hereafter. But be assured that one day He *will* respond. Always be listening for His answer.

God has many layers, and even if He gave us the wisdom to conceive a minute portion of His enormity, our finite and inadequate minds could not fathom His vastness. That's why we must constantly seek out greater knowledge of Him little by little and day by day. Your life will change for the better as you get to know Him more intimately. Each time you communicate with Him, He will reveal Himself to you in deeper ways. In turn, your love for Him will grow because He takes you to the limit and draws you back in to Him again. Then He cleans up your wounds and rewards your faithfulness. Believe it or not, you will be able to appreciate those times. No feeling is greater than when you fight and justice prevails.

So where are you in this spiritual war? Has some crisis stolen your joy? Is fear buzzing around in your ear, whispering from one side to the other about how terrible your life is? To whose voice are you listening? As surely as Satan has sent his messengers to taunt you, God will send His Spirit to minister to you. Invite Him in. He will remind you that everything is still in order and that Jesus and His disciples often healed people who were in crises.

What part of your life needs healing? Is your health in crisis? Are you sick or afflicted in some way? Remember that many of the miracles recorded in the gospels were physical healings of the body. Whether the individuals were lame, bleeding, blind, deaf, or mute; infected with leprosy or dropsy; or even dead—Jesus restored them all. Do you believe that He can do the same for you? That's the source of healing success. He required every person to have faith if they wanted to be healed. Consider the following examples of this fact.

❧

Then Jesus said to the centurion, "Go! It will be done just as you believed it would." And his servant was healed at that very hour. (Matt. 8:13)

Jesus turned and saw her. "Take heart, daughter," He said. "Your faith has healed you." And the woman was healed from that moment. (Matt. 9:22)

Then He touched their eyes and said, "According to your faith will it be done to you;" and their sight was restored. . . . (Matt. 9:29–30)

Hearing this, Jesus said to Jairus, "Don't be afraid; just believe, and she will be healed." (Luke 8:50)

Then He said to him, "Rise and go; your faith has made you well." (Luke 17:19)

Jesus said to him, "Receive your sight, your faith has healed you." (Luke 18:42)

Jesus asked the boy's father, "How long has he been like this?" "From childhood," he answered. "It [a demon] has often thrown him into fire or water to kill him. But if you can do anything, take pity on us and help us." "If you can?" said Jesus. "Everything is possible for him who believes." (Mark 9: 21–23)

❧

It's all about faith. All of those people were afraid for their lives. They were sick in their bodies, demon possessed, or had already tasted death. Yet, He made them whole again. They believed. And Jesus acknowledged that it was their faith that had healed them. Healing was important to Him then, and it has not changed now. In fact, Jesus also gave other people the power to heal because many people were sick and needed attention. Luke 9:1–2 reads, "When Jesus had called the twelve together, He gave them power and authority to drive out all demons and to cure diseases, and He sent them out to preach the kingdom of God and to heal the sick." He had compassion on people who had ailments and wanted them to be released from the sicknesses that had them bound physically and spiritually.

Now, will every person who reads this be healed? Probably not. How God chooses to heal some and not others is beyond me. But you know your own relationship with God. It doesn't mean that your faith is lacking if you are not restored. Perhaps the healing that you desire is not the kind that He chooses. He may feel that you need a different kind of restoration. Perhaps spiritual healing is what's most important for you right now, and He may choose to address that before He addresses the physical. Aren't we more than flesh and blood? Only you and God can determine what the outcome means for your life. But where there is faith, there is no room for fear. And where the Spirit of the Lord is, there is liberty. My hope is that everyone who reads this book will be set free and at peace regardless of what their particular trial might be.

Let's look at another area that is subject to discontentment—your family life. Is it in crisis? Are you afraid that it's falling apart? The family is always under attack. Recently, I heard about an inordinate amount of divorces occurring among my friends. It's heartbreaking for me, so I can only imagine their grief. Longstanding marriages of twenty or more years are being ripped apart, and the reasons for their demise are not frivolous. They are major, and only God can fix them. The simple solution to keeping marriages together should be love. Satan will destroy anything that hints of love, togetherness, devotion, and dedication. After all, the Bible tells us that God is love, and Satan hates God; therefore, he hates anything that remotely resembles God. The family is united in love. Marriages are supposed to be brought together in love, and children are to be produced out of love. Satan wants to destroy all of that.

If you are fearful that he has gotten a foothold in your family and is achieving his goal to destroy it, then dismiss fear as quickly as possible, and rescue your family. Seek God in learning how to repair all of the shattered pieces. If you were united in love from the beginning, He can and will restore what the devil has tried to tear apart.

However, some marriages are doomed to destruction from the start because maybe the union wasn't approved by God in the first place. After years of trying and even praying for its success, you couldn't make it work. Or perhaps somehow through the years, one of you lost sight of God (if ever He was in your line of vision). In either case, marriages cannot survive without God in the midst to keep the spouses bound together. If a love triangle is going to be, let it be among you, your spouse, and God. A marriage takes three, not two.

Another crucial area that is often in crisis in most of our lives involves the financial front. Are you suffering from money woes? Are you having trouble sleeping at night because you're worried about bills? Are you afraid that you won't be able to meet your financial obligations because your income has dried up or is insufficient? I could write a book on this topic alone. But there is no need. Knowledgeable Christian brothers including Larry Burkett and Dwight Nichols have already done this for us. I would encourage you to read their research. But in a nutshell, justice can prevail in this crisis, too, and fear can be squashed.

Jesus teaches us in Matthew 6:25–34 to stop worrying about money and our most basic needs. He says that our Father knows what we need even before we ask Him for it. But seek Him and His righteousness *first,* and He will ensure that we have the resources we need for surviving every day. Cast fear aside. Jesus said, "Don't worry." That's the "don't," but there are some things that we must *do*.

- *Do* become disciplined regarding your finances.
- *Do* the research on how to get out of debt and stay that way.
- *Do* find out what it means to be a good steward in God's eyes.
- *Do* sacrifice to live within your means.
- *Do* find ways to earn a better income.
- *Do* prioritize your life and ensure that money isn't at the top of the list.
- *Do* seek professional financial counseling.
- *Do* pray so that you can sleep well at night.
- *Do* read the Word of God so He can offer you spiritual counseling.
- *Do* seek out a financial ministry that is based on Christian principles.

❧

Remember that God gives to each of us according to our abilities to handle those blessings. He can't keep entrusting you with great financial blessings if you haven't proven to Him that you are capable of using them in the wisest way. He also can't increase your financial blessings if you've demonstrated that you can't handle what you currently receive. Wouldn't you do the same to your children?

Another prime breeding ground for fear is in our physical weaknesses where dependence is a factor. Does relapsing from an addiction that you've tried to kick scare you senseless? You don't want to disappoint the people who love you; more importantly, you don't want to disappoint yourself. But the cravings are becoming unbearable. Or maybe you've already taken a taste and are ashamed. You live each day afraid that this one will be the one that tosses you back into the throes of the life that you've fought so desperately to leave behind. Fear not. You possess the power of the Holy Spirit, and He will not let you fail even if you falter. God provides ways for you to escape temptation if you sincerely don't want to regress. Take yourself out of the situation and find a quiet place to commune with God. Pray as you've never prayed before. If you concentrate on communicating with Him and hearing from Him, you won't have time to think about indulging in the vices that nearly destroyed you before. Don't get scared, become strong and courageous, "Joshua." You are at war!

Since the atrocious acts of September 11, 2001, our safety seems to have moved to the top of the list of fears. Are you afraid for your life as you go about your daily routine, when you travel, or even in your own home? Are you being bullied by someone but you're afraid to stand up to them? Whether you are a child, a teenager, or an adult, it's okay to be afraid of another person, especially if they have threatened to harm us. But read what the Word of God says in Proverbs 29:25: "Fear of man will prove to be a snare, but whoever trusts in the Lord is kept safe." Pray God's protection upon yourself and His hand upon your enemy. I can assure you that the person who is trying to harm you will cease to be a problem. Leave them in God's hand. He is your avenger, and He can fix them in ways that you couldn't imagine. Parents, teach your children to pray for help in sticky situations, too. They should know that even when you're not around, God is always there to protect them.

It's easy for us to fall into the trap of living in anxiety and wondering if evil is lurking around every corner. After all, when you consider that you aren't safe anywhere—whether at home, work, school, the playground, a restaurant, or even church—you have much reason to be wary. But we have too much living to do to spend it in fear. When we come to know and understand God, safety concerns should dissipate. Wisdom about life, death, evil, and God's goodness will take the sting out of all of those things that we fear. In fact, God finds wisdom supreme. According to James 1:5, He'll give you as much wisdom as you desire. Solomon, the wisest of all kings, received wisdom simply because He asked God for it. He also gained riches and honor as a result.

That's how important wisdom is to God. He will give it with riches and honor because it ranks in value right up there with both.

Solomon expands further in Proverbs 3:23–26 on fear and safety when he says, "Then you will go on your way in safety, and your foot will not stumble; when you lie down, you will not be afraid; when you lie down, your sleep will be sweet. Have no fear of sudden disaster or of the ruin that overtakes the wicked, for the Lord will be your confidence and will keep your foot from being snared."

One other major feeding frenzy for fear is in progress. Many people are afraid of moving forward in life. They are afraid that they won't be able to keep up the propulsion necessary to succeed. Have you refused to take on a project because you think it will fail? Or better yet, that it will succeed? Are you afraid to go into business for yourself because it requires getting into debt, and you don't want to take the risk? Fear will keep you where you are all of your life. It will not allow you to progress. It will rob you of the excitement and satisfaction that comes from doing the things that you really enjoy. It takes dreams and pushes them into the backs of closets, beneath beds, at the bottom of briefcases, and anywhere else out of your reach. Fear will tell you that you can't, you shouldn't, and you don't need to. Rebuke it and command it away from your life. Then move toward the urgings of the Spirit of God. He has something special picked out for you. Don't miss out on your blessings because you were afraid to believe that you could do it. I live by my favorite Proverb 16:3: "Commit to the Lord whatever you do and your plans will succeed."

I could go on and on about the areas of our lives that fear chooses to attack. They are usually areas that will affect positive change. Malcolm X was much maligned because he was an advocate of positive change. At a time when Dr. Martin Luther King Jr. was fighting for justice nonviolently, Malcolm's philosophy was "No Justice, No Peace." The hatred that was fueled by fear in the Sixties did not deter Malcolm X. And although some people would not agree with his tactics for attaining justice, he did not shrink from the massive movement for equal rights for blacks in that era. And because he did not allow fear to hinder his fight for justice, African Americans today offer him their respect and gratitude. It's ironic that my son Justice shares the same birthday as Malcolm X, who was always in a fight for justice.

Another man who did not shy away from a fierce fight was Joshua. The Almighty Himself gave Joshua the colossal job of leading the nation of Israel after Moses' death. What a gargantuan and undoubtedly frightening assignment to have! And God knew it. Notice how often the Lord told Joshua to be courageous and not to be afraid.

> After the death of Moses the servant of the Lord, the Lord said to Joshua son of Nun, Moses' aide: "Moses my servant is dead. Now then, you and all these people, get ready to cross the Jordan River into the land I am about to give to them—to the Israelites. I will give you every place where you set your foot as I promised Moses. Your territory will extend from the desert to Lebanon, and from the great river, the Euphrates—all the Hittite country—to the Great Sea on the west. No one will be able to stand up against you all the days of your life. As I was with Moses, so I will be with you; I will never leave you nor forsake you.
>
> "Be strong and courageous, because you will lead these people to inherit the land I swore to their forefathers to give them. Be strong and very courageous. Be careful to obey all the law my servant Moses gave you; do not turn from it to the right or to the left, that you may be successful wherever you go. Do not let this Book of the Law depart from your mouth; meditate on it day and night, so that you may be careful to do everything written in it. Then you will be prosperous and successful. Have I not commanded you? Be strong and courageous. Do not be terrified; do not be discouraged, for the Lord your God will be with you wherever you go." (Joshua 1:1–9)

God promised prosperity and success to Joshua if only he did as he was commanded. What assurance Joshua had! All he needed to do was follow the plan that God had laid out for him. And so should we. We, too, can enjoy prosperity and success if we are as faithful and as obedient as Joshua was. Our circumstances might seem mammoth to us. But imagine Joshua's load. He had to lead God's chosen people into a very special place. The Israelites had been wandering around in the desert for the past forty years, and they numbered in the millions. Now he was being called on to take this mass of people into a sacred place, the Promised Land. And they would have to conquer it first! This would be no walk in the park on a lazy Sunday afternoon. What an awesome responsibility!

Joshua knew how special the Israelites were to God, but he did not shrink in fear from this most important job. In fact, he went into action immediately. He gave orders to the officers of the people and behaved as the leader the Lord knew he was. God gives us certain tasks, duties, and responsibilities because He knows that we can handle them. He doesn't give us these jobs without the instruction and resources to accomplish them. He sees us through them. He often has more faith in us than we have in ourselves. We miss out on blessings because we run and hide when He calls us to serve Him. Before you say no to Him, search out His Spirit. Seek His will. Research His Word. Ask for His guidance.

If we are careful to study the Scripture about Joshua, God outlines a strategy for Joshua to succeed against fear, too. He encouraged him to be strong and courageous. In fact, He says it three times in verses six through nine. Courage and strength were apparently essential elements in accomplishing the job. Therefore, the antithesis of that suggests that allowing fear to weaken him would jeopardize the success of the mission. And what a mission it was. God had made a promise to some people, and He wanted Joshua to help Him carry it out. He was a God of His Word and had always been faithful to keep every promise that He made. Now Joshua had to ensure that he didn't compromise God's track record. Would your knees shake at such a dramatic request?

He also told Joshua to obey the Law. Doing so would keep Joshua right with God. The Law was his moral guide. Today, we should obey not only the Law but also the commands of the Lord Jesus Christ. He gives us guidelines to keep us right and righteous with God so that He can use us to carry out His will. Following the commands that God issued guaranteed Joshua success in all situations, no matter where he found himself.

And finally, God told Joshua to meditate on the Word day and night. We have already established that the Word of God is our weapon. When you read it, it will strengthen you. When you are stronger, your enemies have a harder time fighting you. You weaken them instead. Whenever Satan and his helpers try to discourage you and place fear in your heart by showing you the scary things of this world, you can recall the Word that you read day and night. And you can tell him that his threats are weak because you hold the promises of the Lord God in your head and in your heart.

Joshua took God at His Word and moved into action. He trusted God, and so should we. No matter how big and frightening the circumstance in front of us seems, God promises success if we are obedient to Him. We must go forth boldly and courageously, and peace and prosperity will follow. Joshua obeyed God and ventured forward. He found success in the majority of His battles and ultimately accomplished his mission. He brought the people into the Promised Land—all two million of them—and conquered it. They conquered the land because God was with them, just as He had promised He would be. And He is also with you.

So as I bring this testimony to a close, I would like to encourage you to implement this strategy. You are a fighter even if you are feeling at your weakest. The battle occurs in your spirit. As long as that part of you is strong, you can still succeed. Your resolve to be a faithful follower of the Lord God Almighty and a believer in His Holy Son Jesus Christ will sustain you. You will find hope where it was once abundant but is now depleted. You will discover joy where it once existed but then dried up.

You will find strength that was once dominant but has now waned. Hopefully, you now find fear diminishing in your life. You are recognizing the root cause of it as an evil plot by Satan to trip you up.

Now let's review each strategy to defeat fear individually. Let's bring them all together and discuss them in depth in the next chapter. Read them, study them, implement them, and share them. And watch justice prevail.

Jesus Teaches about the Vine and the Branches (John 15:1–8)

1 I am the true vine, and my Father is the gardener.

2 He cuts off every branch in me that bears no fruit, while every branch that does bear fruit He prunes so that it will be even more fruitful.

3 You are already clean because of the word I have spoken to you.

4 Remain in me, and I will remain in you. No branch can bear fruit by itself; it must remain in the vine. Neither can you bear fruit unless you remain in me.

5 I am the vine; you are the branches. If a man remains in me and I in him, he will bear much fruit; apart from me you can do nothing.

6 If anyone does not remain in me, he is like a branch that is thrown away and withers; such branches are picked up, thrown into the fire and burned.

7 If you remain in me and my words remain in you, ask whatever you wish, and it will be given you.

8 This is to my Father's glory, that you bear much fruit, showing yourselves to be my disciples.

Chapter Five

Strategies that Lead to Victory

N ow the time has come for you to wage war on your enemy fear. You have learned strategies against the backdrop of my own battle against it. I have suffered through the war already and discovered how to defeat it. You don't have to repeat my sufferings because this book has provided the answers for you. Save yourself some heartache and follow the proven strategies that were revealed to me. I have brought them all together in this one chapter along with tactics for implementing each to achieve success. You *must* take action to gain the benefits that I gained. Otherwise, if you've read this entire book and continue to be afraid and worry, then you would have been better off—at least better entertained—reading a novel.

This book is intended to instruct and offer hope. You must *move* to get results. God promised that He'd be with us, but He didn't say that He'd do all of the work for us. Remember Joshua? He was a mighty warrior who was truculent against anyone who would stand in the way of his doing the will of God. He was a brilliant military strategist, and he was faithful to ask God to help him in every battle. And the Lord was faithful to grant him his request.

Let's examine one such military coup of Joshua. In the account of the attack on Ai as recorded in Joshua 8:1–8, we read the following:

> Then the Lord said to Joshua, "Do not be afraid; do not be discouraged. Take the whole army with you, and go up and attack Ai. For I have delivered into your hands the king of Ai, his people, his city and his land. You shall do to Ai and its king as you did to Jericho and its king, except that you may carry off their plunder and livestock for yourselves. Set an ambush behind the city." So Joshua and the whole army moved out to attack Ai. He chose thirty thousand of his best fighting men and sent them out at night with these orders: "Listen carefully. You are to set an ambush behind the city. Don't go very far from it. All of you be on the alert. I and all those with me will advance on the city and when the men come out against us, as they did before, we will flee from them. They will pursue us until we have lured them away from the city, for they will say, 'They are running away from us as they did before.' So when we flee from them, you are to rise up from ambush and take the city. The Lord your God will give it into your hand. When you have taken the city, set it on fire. Do what the Lord has commanded. See to it; you have my orders."

Joshua established a strategy against his enemies so that he could overcome them in a time of battle. He had to outwit them, and God gave him direction on how to do that.

We should approach our battles the same way. Let us transform ourselves from *worriers* into *warriors* because we do not fight our battles alone. We should seek direction from the Lord and ask Him to deliver our enemy into our hands. We need a strategy to build up our forces against our foe so that he won't capitalize on our weaknesses.

Just as God gave Joshua the plan for attacking Ai, I believe that He gave me several strategies against fear. Let me be your Joshua. I will reiterate Joshua's command to his foot soldiers: "Do what the Lord has commanded. See to it, you have my orders." Joshua's orders were for them to do what the Lord commanded; therefore, his orders were God's orders. When we align ourselves with the will of God, our plans will succeed. Proverbs 16:3 tells us that. Seven strategies brought me out on the winning side. I didn't know about them until I was knee deep in terror and felt like a trapped and wounded animal. After the tears subsided and I recovered from the low blow that fear had landed, I realized that I could win. I had no reason to be afraid because I had on my side the One who was in control of all things. He had made many promises to me through His Son, and I believed Him when He said, "Everything is possible for him who believes" (Mark 9:23). Although I was weary, I was still ready to fight, and I responded as the father of the demon-possessed boy did: "I do believe; help me overcome my unbelief!"

This was no time to compromise my faith. Rather, I needed God to *increase* it and to lift me up. I no longer wanted to whine about my woes and misfortunes. God had told me that I could triumph just as He had promised to hand Joshua's enemies over to him. And once I stopped wringing my hands and grieving over my present circumstances, I heard the battle cry of the Lord. I responded to it and, unwittingly, carried out the wishes of the Almighty. Then He brought forth the victory because of my faith.

If you are ready to wage war on fear and fight for the blessings that await you, implement these proven strategies and prevail over your foe. We have discussed them in the previous chapters, but let's look at them individually so that we can see the evidence of their success.

Strategies to Overcome a Scary World

1. Expose your enemy and stand up against it. Never run.
2. Prepare an army for battle. Recruit prayer warriors.
3. Choose your weapons: the shield of faith and your sword, which is God's Word.
4. Establish a strategy against the enemy.
5. Declare war on the enemy, and don't stop fighting until it is defeated.
6. Attack the enemy where it is weak. Use your "sword."
7. Claim the victory and rejoice!

1. EXPOSE YOUR ENEMY AND STAND UP AGAINST IT. NEVER RUN.

This strategy can apply to anything or anyone who has made you an enemy. But for the purpose of this book, we'll address Fear as our archenemy. I had to dig deep beneath the surface of everything that was happening to me to identify Fear as the culprit. A lot was going on, and Fear was able to bury himself beneath all of the chaos. He made his nesting place there and permeated every unfortunate incident to make it seem ten times worse than it really was. Fear is cunning and conniving.

I didn't realize until the ordeal was over that Fear was my biggest opponent. I thought that I was fighting against my own waning faith. But my faith was ebbing only because I was afraid of what I saw and felt happening to me. But for Fear, I would have faired better. My biggest opponent would probably have been Boredom. But I was petrified, and boredom was the least of my complaints. When every day brought contractions, backaches, bleeding, IVs, injections, dips in the baby's heart rate, the threat of infection, the threat of early delivery, nervous medical staff, and fluid leakage rather than buildup, fear was in full effect. But it kept hiding behind my inaccurate assumption that I was losing faith.

So when I read the Word of God, and He reminded me over and over that anything for which I asked in His Son Jesus' name I could receive if I believed and did not doubt, then I was able to challenge Fear. I look back now and realize that I never lost faith. I held God to His Word, and He delivered on His promise. At the time, fear was clouding my judgment, and I thought that I was being a weak Christian. But I never lost hope. And the Bible tells us that hope never disappoints us.

Similarly, you must now expose your enemy and its devious plots. Stand. Do not retreat. Meet him face to face, knowing with certainty that you are already the victor. Amen!

Action Step: Describe your enemy. Who or what are you fighting right now? Think carefully so that you can identify it correctly and avoid being duped by the real enemy. And don't be afraid to consider yourself; sometimes we are our own worst enemies. Also consider that you can be attacked by many enemies at once. Line them up and face them one at a time.

2. PREPARE AN ARMY FOR BATTLE. RECRUIT PRAYER WARRIORS.

Many people, when they are going through tough times, think that they have to keep their problems a secret. They think that it's no one else's business, and they try to go it alone. Or they confide in only a few (who most likely will tell it to someone else anyway). And although I respect everyone's need for privacy, I believe that going it alone sometimes weakens your front-line defense.

When I went into the hospital, I garnered the support of everyone I could get. My husband recruited those in his ranks as well. We were all in one accord, and we prayed incessantly day and night. I volunteered information about my condition because I wanted them to pray for specific things. I needed them to pray that I would make it to week twenty-eight and beyond. I needed them to pray that my child would be born with no complications. I needed them to pray for the wisdom of the doctors and medical staff, and that they wouldn't make any hasty moves.

We gathered so many recruits that we always had someone offering up a petition for me. My church family of more than 4,400 souls interceded for me. I was listed in the church bulletin's "Sick and Shut In" section. As a result, we were lifted in prayer every Sunday at all services.

Then I had a wonderful, caring trio—my pastor, his wife, and the assistant pastor—who came regularly to see me. In addition to the rest of the church family's praying, the deacons from my church also came to my hospital room and brought me Communion. Even after my immediate release, they met me in the waiting area outside of the NICU to offer me the holy sacraments and to lift my family in prayer before I'd go in to see Justice on Sunday mornings.

My husband and I prayed every day as he came to be with me by my bedside. He read Scripture to me, brought tapes of the church services that I missed, and tried to bring friends by to keep me uplifted. No one knew how frightened I was because when they came into the room I always wore a smile–not to hide anything but because I was happy to see them. Although I was shaky on the inside, I was comforted every time a visitor stopped in and spoke an encouraging word.

Another group of warriors were my customers who sent prayers and care packages. They checked in with me regularly throughout my ordeal and welcomed me with open arms when I returned to work. My co-workers did the same, and one of them was always placing a call for an update to pass on to the others. One special co-worker/friend had her choir in California "wailing" for my family and me—not in song, but in prayer. They cried out to God on our behalf just as Jesus had done. A relative doing a stint in a Louisiana detention center (whose life is so dramatically changed by God that it warrants a book in itself) had the entire prison ministry praying for us.

And, of course, my blood family—my sisters, aunts, cousins, in-laws, nieces, nephews, brothers, uncles, and stepchildren—were all lifting me up day in and day out. Even those who were not blood related but are as close to me as if we came from the same genes came with prayers on their hearts (and food, too, which was a blessing indeed).

The most memorable prayer came from one of my doctors when I was having a particularly challenging day. That was so special to me, and I pray God's blessings upon him and his family for taking that bold step. It did wonders for my faith. And I mustn't forget the nurses in the high-risk obstetrics unit who audibly praised God during some very scary moments when they couldn't locate the baby's heartbeat.

Oh, what a united front we were! Could God ignore such a wealth of petitions? His Word says no. Actually, all He requires is that two or three to be gathered in the name of Jesus. This baby and I were *covered* in prayer. There was no way He would deny such diligent requests.

So whatever your challenge, gather up as many believers as you can. Recruit strong prayer warriors as foot soldiers. Ask them to take up their arms (the Word) against the enemy that you have identified from Strategy #1. Then ask them to intercede for you. Ask them to pray as Jesus did on the Mount of Olives until they perspire and it resembles drops of blood. God rewards earnest prayer. And you don't have to compromise your privacy to reap the benefits of righteous petitions.

Action Step: List prayer warriors who will stand on the front lines with you. Call them and prepare them for battle. Choose specific areas for prayer that will help you beat the adversary. Ask them to pray particularly for those things.

3. Choose your weapons: the shield of faith and the sword, which is God's Word.

Ephesians 6:10–18 describes the armor of God. Paul wrote to the Ephesians encouraging them to put on the full armor of God so that they could take a stand against the Devil's schemes. He warns us that our battle is spiritual, not physical. You may be struggling in the flesh right now, especially where fear has taken hold. But you can dress in full gear against dark powers. And any weapon that evil shoots your way will fizzle out once it bangs against your mighty shield of faith. Paul says, "Therefore put on the full armor of God, so that when the day of evil comes, you may be able to stand your ground, and after you have done everything to stand" (v. 13).

The day of evil can come at any moment. That's why we are always to be prepared. We should always be dressed from head to toe and ready to do battle with the enemy. Truth, righteousness, peace, faith, and salvation are all of the weapons you need. Paul warns us to be alert. As I mentioned earlier, you will not always be given notice of impending hardship. Evil most often catches us when we least expect it. That's how it knocks us to our knees. But while we're down there, all we have to do is pray. Then rise above it with the might that comes from being ready and alert.

Your weapons might also be fairness, equality, strength, wisdom, knowledge, joy, praise, and hope. You may choose a cool and even temper and a bridled tongue in your war. No matter what the battle is, arm yourself with the appropriate weapons to cut the enemy down and lift up the wishes of the Lord.

I took up arms immediately, even as the water first gushed down my legs. This was undoubtedly a time for prayer. I was thrust into battle, so I raised my shield of faith and asked God to intervene as I forged ahead against the shots fired upon me. I asked Him to save my child. I asked Him to honor His promises. And then I believed. The Word says that we need only a mustard seed of faith. Even at my weakest moments, I had more than that. I put my faith in front of me as a shield of protection against fear and doubt. As a believer, I learned over the years to walk by faith and not by sight. When I looked at what fear was showing me, it weakened me. So we should not always function based on what we see. Sometimes we must take our eyes off the circumstances before us and look toward heaven. We have to believe that a greater power and purpose are at work beyond what is in our sight.

While I held up my shield, I picked up my sword and fought fear with it. I wielded the Word of God like a weapon that could cut down any enemy. Hebrews 4:12 describes it as a double-edged sword: "It is living and active. It penetrates even to dividing soul and spirit, joints and marrow; it judges the thoughts and attitudes of the heart." I used it to stab fear, to annihilate it. I opened my Bible every day and read God's guarantees. His Word was like a salve on an open wound. It healed me and eased my pain. It encouraged me and enlightened me. It renewed my hope every day, and at the same time it was destroying my enemy.

When fear eased in as the darkness fell, I pulled out the Word and dared the enemy to challenge me on it. Whatever lies fear told me about my circumstances, I was able to combat them with the Truth, which can be found only in the Word of God.

For example, when fear said, "Your little Justice will die. Look at these other babies in here suffering and dying all around you. What makes you think God won't allow the same for your son? Give up on serving Him now."

I whipped out my sword from its sheath and fought back with Luke 18:7: "And will not God bring about justice for His chosen ones, who cry out to Him day and night? Will He keep putting them off?" This is what I meant in an earlier chapter when I said that I didn't realize how prophetic my child's name would be. When we chose his name even before this crisis occurred, little did I know that God would speak to me directly— even going so far as to mention "justice" by name—to reassure me through His Word. The Word is the most powerful weapon in spiritual warfare. Carry it with you as if your spiritual life depended on it.

Action Step: Research Scripture to arm yourself against the enemy. Find as many reassuring promises as you can. Jot them down where you can refer to them easily during your most trying moments. Commit to memory your favorite passages in case you find yourself without your weapon physically.

4. ESTABLISH A STRATEGY AGAINST THE ENEMY.

Your strategy is to follow the steps that I am listing for you now. They are proven. I am a witness that they work, and I have evidence to prove it—my beautiful son, Justice. The tactics that I used for making this strategy successful were prophecy, prayer, and praise. You may use different tactics. But whatever you do, have tactics and use them. Prophecy is a gift that my pastor and I discovered I have when we profiled my strengths as a Christian. I enjoy indulging in the Word of God and then sharing it with whomever I can, and that's an act of evangelizing. In the profile, the gift of prophecy was akin to evangelism and preaching. I used my gift of prophecy during this fight to tell others about the goodness of God and the plots of the Evil One. It turned others toward the Lord and against Satan—directly opposite of the effect that the Devil was trying to accomplish. This was the first tactic in my strategy against the enemy.

The second tactic was my most effective one—prayer. Prayer is like a bullet. It can be released at any time, anywhere, and hit its target. I was in constant communication with God, as were others on my behalf, and He granted us our request. We struck down fear.

Finally, praise should be offered whether you've finished the battle or are in the midst of it. It's another weapon, an excellent tactic against fear. Fear will be perplexed by your ability to offer up praises unto God even (especially) when you are downtrodden and in despair. And God will rejoice with you because you praised Him anyhow. He rewards such unselfish worship best of all. It helps you personally to sing, shout, dance, or lift up holy hands as an offering unto the Lord. It confirms your belief and solidifies your faith. You'll actually be able to embrace the victory more readily, even before you achieve it.

Action Step: Put this strategy into effect. Pray for further guidance on how to plan it and implement it to the utmost. Write down tactics for completing each step. Choose your own according to your particular struggle. Then take action.

5. DECLARE WAR ON THE ENEMY, AND DON'T STOP FIGHTING UNTIL IT IS DEFEATED.

Now, charge! Run down fear; smoke it out of its hiding place. Don't allow it to build up until it stifles you and causes you to live a life that is less than what you can have. God promised us great things, things beyond what our finite minds could even imagine. Remember Ephesians 3:30: ". . . to Him who is able to do immeasurably more than all we ask or imagine according to His power that is at work within us. . . ." Yet, each day, we miss our blessings or skimp on them because we are afraid that we can't have those pie-in-the-sky dreams. We think that it's a ridiculous notion although we long to make them come true. Or somebody tells us that it'll never happen for us. Why not? People live their dreams every day. Why can't it happen for *us?*

One caveat, however: don't let your dreams be money driven. That can lead easily to greed and selfishness. Money and material possessions do not make life fulfilling. Ask anyone who has a lot of it. They surely have other more important things missing in their lives that money can't buy. Material abundance should only be *lagniappe*—a Cajun word that means "a little something extra." But if it doesn't come, your life shouldn't be any worse off. God has other great things in store for you. All you have to do is ask Him for them and believe that you will receive them.

Fear will tell you that because you don't deserve them, they aren't yours to have. *None* of us deserves *anything* that God gives us. But He still offers to provide us with gifts that add to the enjoyment of our lives. So cast aside fear and embrace all of the blessings that God has set aside for you. Remember, fear is a thief. It will steal your peace. But fight it. And don't give up the fight until you are sure that you have your foot on its neck.

Although I never stopped fighting, I sometimes got tired. When it didn't look like I'd make it to week thirty-four as I would have liked, I got tired of straining toward that goal. When the contractions started and didn't seem to want to cease, I grew tired of trying to calm them. When my body ached from lying in one position in an uncomfortable bed, I felt fatigue. But I never gave up. I said to myself, *This is for my son. Whatever is necessary, I will do. I have power through the Lord Jesus. I can do all things through Him because He strengthens me.* I grew tired, but I did not give in. At least not to the enemy. I often relinquished the fight to my Lord. To Him I would say, "Lord, whatever be your will. I am tired. Let your will be done." That was when I discovered success.

The craziness ceased and the evil dissipated for a while. God's Holy Spirit built me up from the inside and helped me get ready for the next battle. It was like fighting in a boxing ring and hearing the bell. I would go to my corner kind of banged up, but the Holy Spirit would be waiting there for me to give me the pep talk that I needed and to nurse my wounds. He would remind me that I had been promised the victory. God had said it in His Word: "And without faith it is impossible to please God, because anyone who comes to Him must believe that He exists and that He rewards those who earnestly seek Him."

Action Step: Take action. Do not sit in despair. *Do* something. Get angry, get determined, get busy—but do *something*. You are at war! What additional steps would you take now?

6. Attack the enemy where it is weak.

Depending on what or who your enemy is, you must discover its weakness. Trust me—your enemy is searching for your weakness if it doesn't already know what it is. Because we have established in this book the fact that fear is the enemy, we must discover its weakness. What I've found is that faith can defeat fear. Fear buckles under when a person possesses a strong conviction for God's promises.

The greater your faith, the smaller your fear. Where there is faith, there should be no fear. Therefore, fear's weakness is being unable to stand against a believer who has faith. It cannot. No room exists for the coexistence of both faith and fear. As was mentioned in Strategy #3, faith is a shield to protect us against all manner of evil. When I attacked fear with faith, I knocked its foundation right out from under it. Then the whole wall of fear that was built up in this war began to crumble. Fear could not stand up under the weight of even a mustard seed-sized faith. Do you know how tiny a mustard seed is? It's minuscule. But it might as well be a tank, a cannon, or a bazooka. It is the greatest defense against fear.

Discover your enemy's weakness, and immediately gather the weapons necessary to do battle. You must choose your weapons carefully if they are to be effective in bringing about the defeat of your enemy. Your enemy's weaknesses might not be apparent immediately. But God knows the weaknesses of each of us, especially of evil things. Ask Him to direct you on how to arm yourself against your enemy. Ask Him to help you choose the most effective weapon.

Sometimes our enemies might have more than one weakness. Great! That gives us even more areas in which to attack him and bring him to his knees. Attack him viciously, and, as in Strategy #5, don't stop until he succumbs.

Action Step: Identify and list the weaknesses of your enemy. Then describe how you will attack in those areas.

And finally. . . .

7. Claim the victory and rejoice!

Once you have the right weapons, the right strategy, and the right people in your corner, you can shout the victory. There is no taste of defeat. There isn't even a consideration that defeat is even a remote possibility. Even before the final blow is struck, you should cry out with a voice of praise because you know that you have won. As with David, believe that God has always been on your side, and there's no way you can lose. First Samuel 18:14 says, "In everything he [David] had great success, because the Lord was with him." And so it can and should be with you—and with all believers.

David found his strength in God, just as we should. And he defeated many enemies and conquered great lands because he followed the leading of the Lord God, just as Joshua had done. But David enjoyed praising God, and he did so without shame. In fact, he did so with great boldness. Second Samuel 6:14–15 tells us that he danced before the Lord "with all of his might" when he brought up the ark of God to the city of David. There were shouts and the sounds of trumpets. There was dancing, singing, and shouting in the streets. It was contagious.

Today, I am still dancing. I am still rejoicing. And I anticipate that I will be doing so for the rest of my life. My son will rejoice when he becomes old enough to appreciate the blessing that the Lord gave him. And as I anticipate even greater things from God, I continue to celebrate. I celebrate the past victories, and I celebrate the victories that are on the way.

Go ahead. Claim the victory. Even as you are going through the war, thank God in advance for what He is going to do. If He has promised you victory, thank Him for it just as you would thank any friend who said that he or she would take care of a problem that you couldn't handle. Act as if you've already won—even if you are in the thick of things.

Once you have indeed won, sing, shout, dance, cry, or clap—do whatever you choose as a praise offering unto the Lord. He deserves it. You could never match His outstanding blessing with outstanding praise, but He is happy for your gratitude. Dance as David did! Such rejoicing is pleasing to the Lord; He is to be glorified.

Now that you have the strategy, a proven strategy, to wage war against fear and win, read the final chapter to gather tools from the war chest. These will make your efforts effective. It is time for you to take action. It is time for you to win back peace in your life and move forward to attain the blessings that God has for you.

The Best Is Yet to Come
(2 Corinthians 2:9)

However, as it is written:

"No eye has seen,

no ear has heard,

no mind has conceived

what God has prepared for those who love Him."

Chapter Six

Weapons from the War Chest

In battle, you must always use the most effective weapons to bring your enemies to their knees. I have noted throughout this book that the most effective weapons against fear are the shield of faith and the sword, which is the Word of God. In this chapter, you will find Scripture with which you can polish your sword and make your enemy tremble. I have also included seven prayers that you can pray when you don't have the words yourself. Sometimes we feel too downtrodden to pray in the heat of battle. Hopefully, these prayers will speak to your situation and help you win the war. Fight on!

Prayers Against Fear

Dear God,

    With great humility I come to you confused and in despair. I am afraid. I ask that you would remove this stifling feeling from my heart and my body. Take away the trembling and trepidation. Please replace them with confidence and courage. I know that I don't have to be afraid because you have promised to be with me all of the days of my life. And although the world around me seems to be crazy, scary, and out of control, remind me that you have calmed an angry sea. You sent a boy to defeat a giant, and you've shut the mouths of ferocious lions. No matter what frightens me, it can be squelched under your mighty hand. I thank you now for restoring my courage. I thank you for increasing my faith. In the powerful name of Jesus, I pray. Amen.

Almighty Father,

    I praise you for your goodness and your loving kindness. I know that sometimes hardships come our way to make us strong. This one is particularly difficult for me, and I am afraid. I know that I don't have to be, but I find it hard to beat this enemy. Please remove fear from my heart. Let me not fret over what is to come. Increase my faith so that I will trust only in you that you will do what is best for me. I praise you now for lifting the heavy burden of fear from my shoulders. I accept the release of its grasp from around my neck. I thank you for the positive outcome of the situation and the strength to accept even the hard lessons I have to learn. I cast all of my cares upon you. In Christ I pray. Amen.

Most Gracious God,

I ask that you empower me on this day at this moment against my enemy, fear. He is like a lion seeking whom he can devour, and he has quite a hold on me between his teeth. I pray for relief and a release from his strong hold. I don't know what the future holds for me in this battle, but I pray that you are with me throughout so that in the end I will prevail. I pray that you give me the strength I need to make it through without failing. I ask that you reveal to me the most valuable lesson I am to learn so that I may share it with others. I give you the glory for being a God who is all powerful and who wants to empower His people. I receive your power within my spirit right now. I pray that I am able to hear your urgings and will be obedient to your guidance. Please grant me peace in my spirit now so that the enemy will not weaken me. In the holy name of Jesus I pray. Amen.

Glorious God,

I celebrate you through my trials. I am struggling and suffering greatly at this moment, but I believe that you will bring me through this the victor. I am hurting and in despair, Lord, but I know that the day is coming when I will be able to rejoice about all that you've done. I trust in you, Lord, and I know that you are near me. You said that you'd never leave me nor forsake me. You never have, although I've sometimes cast you aside or might have even turned my back on you for a period of time. Thank you for receiving me back and for wiping the slate clean. It is so good to have a shoulder on which to lean when no one else seems to know what to do. Thank you for listening to my fears and my concerns. And most of all, thank you for soothing my hurts and giving me the hope of triumph that awaits me in the end. I receive the blessings that are on the way right now. I will believe and not doubt that all will be well when this battle is over and I am left standing. In the power-filled name of Jesus I pray. Amen.

Heavenly Father,

I need your help. I am helpless and almost hopeless. Restore me during these difficult times. I don't have the energy to pray. My shoulders are trembling under the weight of my grief. Please bring me peace and strengthen me in the end. I will give you all of the glory for all that you've done and serve as a witness to your awesome power. In the righteous name of Jesus, Amen.

Most Holy God,

Fear is ever pounding on my heart and in my mind, but I want to be courageous and strong like Joshua. Give me that strength. Give me the courage I need. I cannot fight this battle alone. Neither do I want to attempt it alone. I know that I can win with you on my side. I will not accept defeat. Although the circumstances before me look hopeless, I will never lose hope. And even if the outcome is not what I'd like it to be, please help me to remember that it is your will that must be done. Help me through my grief, and please take these cares from me. I find them hard to release on my own. Remind me of your promises in your Word, and lead me to Scriptures that will speak to me. I need to hear from you. Let me distinguish your voice from so many others and be obedient to your leading. In the blessed name of Jesus I pray. Amen.

Most High God,

Who can defeat you? No one. Who can honor his word better than you? No one. Who is more powerful than you? Not a single soul. I lift your name on high and sing your praises. You have delivered many other people who were in dire situations before me, and you have also delivered me more times than I can remember. You have always been there for me even when I haven't been grateful to you. And I know that you are still offering yourself to me. Thank you, Lord. Please allow your Holy Spirit to refresh me and remind me that I am victorious in you. Through this battle that I'm fighting, the victory is already mine. I just need to keep on fighting and never give up. Please strengthen me to be able to do just that. I need you now, and I receive your answers to these requests, in the Name of your Son Jesus. Amen.

Scriptures Against Fear

1 Chronicles 28:20

David also said to Solomon his son, "Be strong and courageous, and do the work. Do not be afraid or discouraged, for the Lord God, my God, is with you. He will not fail you or forsake you until all the work for the service of the temple of the Lord is finished."

⸎

Psalm 27:1–3

The Lord is my light and my salvation—
Whom shall I fear?
The Lord is the stronghold of my life—
Of whom shall I be afraid?
When evil men advance against me
To devour my flesh,
When my enemies and my foes attack me,
They will stumble and fall.
Though an army besiege me,
My heart will not fear;
Though war break out against me,
Even then will I be confident.

⸎

Mark 4:40

He [Jesus] said to His disciples, "Why are you so afraid? Do you still have no faith?"

Luke 12:4–5

I tell you, my friends, do not be afraid of those who kill the body and after that can do no more. But I will show you whom you should fear: Fear Him who, after the killing of the body, has power to throw you into hell. Yes, I tell you, fear Him.

Psalm 23:4

Even though I walk
Through the valley of the shadow of death,
I will fear no evil,
For you are with me;
Your rod and your staff,
They comfort me.

Proverbs 3:23–26

Then you will go on your way in safety,
And your foot will not stumble;
When you lie down, you will not be afraid;
When you lie down, your sleep will be sweet.
Have no fear of sudden disaster
Or of the ruin that overtakes the wicked,
For the Lord will be your confidence
And will keep your foot from being snared.

James 4:7
Submit yourselves, then, to God. Resist the devil, and he will flee from you.

John 14:1
Do not let your hearts be troubled. Trust in God; trust also in me [Jesus].

John 14: 27
Peace I leave with you; my peace I give you. I do not give as the world gives. Do not let your hearts be troubled and do not be afraid.

John 16:33
I [Jesus] have told you these things, so that in me you may have peace. In this world you will have trouble. But take heart! I have overcome the world.

Justice Parker

To order additional copies of

WAGING WAR ON FEAR

Have your credit card ready and call
Toll free: (877) 421-READ (7323)
or send $12.00* each plus $4.95 S&H** to

WinePress Publishing
PO Box 428
Enumclaw, WA 98022

or order online at: www.winepresspub.com

*WA residents, add 8.4% sales tax
**add $1.50 S&H for each additional book ordered